In the Presence of Taxes:

Applications of After-tax
Asset Valuations

In the Presence of Taxes:
Applications of After-tax Asset Valuations

William Reichenstein, Ph.D., CFA®

The Financial Planning Association (FPA) is the membership association for the financial planning community. FPA is committed to providing information and resources to help financial planners and those who champion the financial planning process succeed. FPA believes that everyone needs objective advice to make smart financial decisions.

FPA Press is the publishing arm of FPA, providing current content and advanced thinking on technical and practice management topics.

Information in this book is accurate at the time of publication and consistent with the standards of good practice in the financial planning community. As research and practice advance, however, standards may change. For this reason, it is recommended that readers evaluate the applicability of any recommendation in light of particular situations and changing standards.

Financial Planning Association
4100 Mississippi Ave., Suite 400
Denver, Colorado 80246-3053

Phone: 800.322.4237
Fax: 303.759.0749
E-mail: FPApress@FPAnet.org

www.FPAnet.org

Copyright © 2008 FPA Press. All rights reserved.

ISBN: 0-9798775-1-2
ISBN-13 978-0-9798775-1-3

Manufactured in the United States of America

To my wife, Mineva.

About the Author

William Reichenstein, Ph.D., CFA®, has held the Pat and Thomas R. Powers Chair in Investment Management at Baylor University since 1990. He has a long history of service to the profession. He is on the Editorial Review Board of *Journal of Financial Planning*, the Advisory Board of *Journal of Wealth Management*, an Associate Editor of *Journal of Investing*, Contributing Editor-Portfolio Management for American Association of Individual Investors' *AAII Journal*, and on the Editorial Board of *Journal of Financial Education*. He has been named a TIAA-CREF Fellow, which is a title given to select scholars who have best contributed to retirement and other research of interest to TIAA-CREF's academic clientele. From August 2005 through August 2008, he served as a member of Private Wealth Advisory Committee of CFA Institute. He has served as president of the Southwestern Finance Association, and served two terms as Associate Editor of *Financial Services Review*.

Dr. Reichenstein has written more than 130 articles for professional and academic journals. He is a frequent contributor to *AAII Journal*, *Financial Analysts Journal*, *Journal of Financial Planning*, *Journal of Investing*, *Journal of Portfolio Management*, and *Journal of Wealth Management*. He has received numerous research and teaching awards, including the 2008 Financial Frontiers Editors' Choice Award for some of his work discussed in this book. He has spoken at numerous professional and academic conferences. His work has been discussed in the *Wall Street Journal*, *Barron's*, *Forbes*, *Smart Money*, and elsewhere, and he is frequently quoted in newspapers throughout this country.

For the past decade, his work has concentrated on two themes. The first theme, which is the subject of this book, concerns the intersection of taxes and investments. For example, how does the choice of savings vehicles—Roth IRA, 401(k), or taxable account—affect the percent of pre-tax returns received by and pre-tax risk borne by an individual investor? How do the relative sizes of the marginal tax rates this year and in retirement affect the choice between saving in a Roth 401(k) or a 401(k)? How should we adjust assets' market values for embedded tax liabilities when calculating an after-tax asset allocation? For example, an individual with $1 million in bonds in a 401(k) and $1 million in stocks in a Roth IRA does not have a 50 percent bonds and 50 percent stock asset allocation because the *pre-tax* dollars in the 401(k) are smaller than the *after-tax* dollars in the Roth IRA. The second theme is that financial advisers should manage an individual's extended portfolio, where the extended portfolio might contain financial assets plus other non-financial assets such as defined-benefit plans, Social Security, and human capital.

About FPA

The Financial Planning Association® (FPA®) is the membership organization for the financial planning community. FPA is built around four Core Values—Competence, Integrity, Relationships, and Stewardship. We want as members those who share our core values.

FPA's primary aim is to be the community that fosters the value of financial planning and advances the financial planning profession. The FPA strategy to accomplish its objectives involves welcoming all those who advance the financial planning process and promoting the CERTIFIED FINANCIAL PLANNER™ (CFP®) marks as the cornerstone of the financial planning profession. FPA is the heart of financial planning, connecting those who deliver, support, and benefit from it.

FPA was created on the foundation that the CFP marks best represent the promise and the future of the financial planning profession. CFP certification offers the public a consistent and credible symbol of professional competence in financial planning. And FPA benefits the public by helping to ensure that financial planning is delivered through competent, ethical financial planners.

FPA members include individuals and companies who are dedicated to helping people make wise financial decisions to achieve their life goals and dreams. FPA believes that everyone needs objective advice to make smart financial decisions and that when seeking the advice of a financial planner, the planner should be a CFP professional.

FPA is committed to improving and enhancing the professional lives and capabilities of our members. We offer a variety of programs and services to that end.

Table of Contents

Introduction 1

Chapter 1: Introduction and Rationale of
Calculating an After-tax Asset Allocation 5

Chapter 2: Principal, Risk, and Returns Sharing
across Savings Vehicles 13

Chapter 3: How to Calculate an After-tax
Asset Allocation 27

Chapter 4: Choice of Savings Vehicles When
Saving for Retirement 43

Chapter 5: Mean Variance Optimization and
Asset Location with Taxes 59

Chapter 6: Withdrawal Strategies to Make Your
Nest Egg Last Longer 75

Chapter 7: Summary and More. 99

Appendix A: Theoretical Arguments Associated
with Calculating Assets' After-tax Values 105

Appendix B: Estimating Marginal Tax Rates
in Retirement 111

Appendix C: After-tax Valuation of Assets
Held in Taxable Accounts and Non-qualified
Annuities with Built-in Deferred Returns 119

References 123

Index 125

Introduction

This book is my attempt to succinctly combine in one source my thinking about many issues related to taxes and private wealth management. My prior work, often written with William Jennings, has been published in *Financial Services Review, Journal of Financial Planning, Journal of Wealth Management, Financial Analysts Journal,* (American Association of Individual Investors) *AAII Journal,* or published by TIAA-CREF Institute or John Wiley & Sons. This book not only brings together this material, but it also explains how many of the issues are interconnected. It provides a consistent framework that is used to address several wealth management issues.

For example, this book begins by explaining why a dollar in a tax-deferred account such as a 401(k) is like $(1 - t_n)$ dollar in a tax-exempt account such as a Roth IRA, where t_n is the expected tax rate in retirement. For someone who will be in the 25 percent tax bracket in retirement, $1 in a 401(k) is like $0.75 in a Roth IRA because, if invested in the same asset, they will each purchase the same amount of goods and services when withdrawn in retirement. This key concept is developed in the first two chapters. It has implications for: 1) the calculation of an individual's asset allocation, 2) the asset location decision, which is defined later, and 3) preferred withdrawal sequence from the savings vehicles in retirement. Each of these topics is covered in a later chapter.

For example, Chapter 3 explains how to calculate an after-tax asset allocation. We first convert assets' market values to after-tax values and then calculate the asset allocation using these after-tax values. The traditional approach to calculating an individual's asset allocation ignores taxes and thus considers $1 of *pre-tax* funds in a 401(k) to be equivalent to $1 of *after-tax* funds in a Roth IRA. In contrast, the after-tax approach to calculating an individual's asset allocation recognizes that taxes exist and considers each pre-tax dollar to be smaller than each after-tax dollar. In short, the *after-tax* asset allocation compares *after-tax* funds in a 401(k) to *after-tax* funds in a Roth IRA or other savings vehicle.

Chapter 4 helps individuals select the best savings vehicles when saving for retirement. When given the choice, should the individual save in a Roth IRA or a traditional IRA? A key factor in the decision is usually a comparison between today's marginal tax rate and the expected marginal tax rate when the funds will be withdrawn in retirement. However, other factors are important, especially when the two marginal tax rates are close.

Chapter 5 illustrates differences between a traditional tax-oblivious mean variance optimization and an after-tax mean variance optimization. In addition, the optimal asset *location* decision follows directly from after-tax mean variance optimization, where asset *location* refers to the decision to locate stocks in taxable accounts and bonds in tax-deferred accounts and Roths, or vice versa. For example, consider an individual who has funds in both a 401(k) and a taxable account. He has a target asset allocation of bonds and stocks. While attaining his target asset allocation, should he *locate* bonds in the 401(k) and stocks in the taxable account, or vice versa? As we shall see, the framework developed in this book makes it easy to explain his optimal asset location decision is to hold bonds in the 401(k) and stocks in the taxable account, while attaining his target asset allocation.

Chapter 6 discusses withdrawal strategies during retirement. Suppose a retiree has funds in tax-deferred accounts, Roth IRAs, and taxable accounts. This chapter considers whether she should withdraw funds from taxable accounts first followed by tax-deferred accounts and then Roth IRAs or whether another sequence would be preferred. By withdrawing funds in a tax-savvy manner, a retiree may be able to extend her portfolio's longevity by a few years.

The final chapter presents a brief summary of the key principles and investment implications developed in the book. In addition, it discusses related literature that goes beyond the material covered in this book.

This book also contains three appendixes. Appendixes A and C present the development of thought related to the calculation of assets' after-tax values, which are used to calculate an after-tax asset allocation. Appendix B discusses issues related to the estimation of marginal tax rates in retirement.

Each chapter contains a brief introduction. At the end of each chapter, a summary section presents a list of the principles and investment implications established in that chapter.

This book does not provide a history of the development of thought related to each topic discussed in this book.[1] Rather, it provides my thinking about key issues and a consistent framework for addressing each of these key issues. As in any field, this work builds on and benefits from the work of many other scholars. A partial list of these scholars includes: Jean Brunel, Harold Evensky, Robert Gordon, Stephen Horan, Jeffrey Horvitz, William Jennings, Deena Katz, Moshe Milevsky, James Poterba, Douglas Rogers, John Shoven, Clemens Sialm, William Sibley, Sandeep Singh, John Spitzer, and Jarrod Wilcox. Appendix A discusses key articles by Horan and Sibley on the issue of calculating an individual's after-tax asset allocation. Appendix C explains how to calculate the after-tax value of assets with embedded tax-deferred returns, such as stocks with unrealized capital gains. My ideas build on the work and models of Stephen Horan, and this material would not have been possible without his prior work. But, again, this book is not intended to be a history of the development of thought on these and other issues.

I conclude with special thanks to special people. As noted earlier, William Jennings has co-authored many of my articles and books in this area and should share equally in the credit. Even though Stephen Horan and I sometimes disagree on specific issues, through a series of discussions and exchanges he has helped me develop my thoughts and clarify my idea. I value his work and friendship. I thank Mary Corbin and Peggy Doviak for their valuable suggestions for improving this book. Finally, I thank my wife, Mineva, for her endless support and encouragement.

ENDNOTE

[1]Although it does not provide a complete bibliography of this prior literature, the interested reader should see Jennings and Reichenstein, *The Literature of Private Wealth Management*, Research Foundation of the CFA Institute, 2006, www.cfapubs.org/doi/pdf/10.2470/rflr.v1.n3.4362. This annotated bibliography provides references to many of the most important works related to private wealth management.

1 | *Introduction and Rationale of Calculating an After-tax Asset Allocation*

In thinking about taxes and private wealth management, it's important to have a consistent framework that addresses several wealth management issues. This chapter introduces a key insight: $1 in a tax-deferred account such as a 401(k) is like $(1 - t_n)$ dollar in a Roth IRA, where t_n is the expected tax rate in retirement. This insight has implications for: 1) the portions of returns received by and risk borne by individual investors in a tax-deferred account, 2) the calculation of an individual's asset allocation, 3) the optimal asset-location decision, and 4) the optimal withdrawal sequence from the savings vehicles in retirement. Each of these topics is covered in a later chapter. But this key insight is presented in this chapter and further developed in Chapter 2.

Table 1.1. Savings in 401(k) and Roth IRA		
Savings Vehicle	**Original Investment**	**Retirement Wealth**
Roth IRA	$7,500 after-tax funds	$30,000 after-tax funds
401(k)	$10,000 pre-tax funds (or $7,500 after-tax funds)	$40,000 pre-tax funds <u>– $10,000 taxes</u> $30,000 after-tax funds

The individual will have a marginal tax rate of 25 percent in retirement.

KEY INSIGHT

Table 1.1 presents Peggy's portfolio. She is single, age 50, and saving for retirement. She expects to have a 25 percent marginal tax rate in retirement. She has $7,500 of *after-tax* funds in a Roth IRA, $10,000 of *pre-tax* funds in a 401(k), and they are invested in the same asset. That underlying asset could be stocks, bonds, or a mutual fund. Without loss of generality, let's assume it is a stock fund and its value will quadruple by the time the funds are withdrawn in retirement. The Roth IRA will be worth $30,000 after taxes, so she can withdraw the funds and buy $30,000 of goods and services. The 401(k) will be worth $40,000 of pre-tax funds, or $30,000 after taxes at withdrawal. She can withdraw the funds and buy $30,000 of goods and services.

Table 1.2 assumes the underlying investment doubles between now and withdrawal in retirement. In this case, the Roth IRA will be worth $15,000 after taxes and the 401(k) will

Table 1.2. Savings in 401(k) and Roth IRA		
Savings Vehicle	**Original Investment**	**Retirement Wealth**
Roth IRA	$7,500 after-tax funds	$15,000 after-tax funds
401(k)	$10,000 pre-tax funds (or $7,500 after-tax funds)	$20,000 pre-tax funds <u>– $5,000 taxes</u> $15,000 after-tax funds

The individual will have a marginal tax rate of 25 percent in retirement.

Table 1.3. Savings in 401(k) and Roth IRA		
Savings Vehicle	**Original Investment**	**Retirement Wealth**
Roth IRA	$7,500 after-tax funds	$3,750 after-tax funds
401(k)	$10,000 pre-tax funds (or $7,500 after-tax funds)	$5,000 pre-tax funds −$1,250 taxes $3,750 after-tax funds

The individual will have a marginal tax rate of 25 percent in retirement.

be worth $20,000 before taxes, but $15,000 after taxes. They will each buy $15,000 of goods and services in retirement.

Table 1.3 assumes the underlying asset loses 50 percent between now and withdrawal in retirement. The Roth IRA and 401(k) would each be worth $3,750 after taxes, and could purchase this amount of goods and services. In short, no matter what the asset's rate of return, $10,000 of pre-tax funds in a 401(k) will buy the same amount of goods and services as $7,500 of after-tax funds in a Roth IRA.

These examples lead to the following conclusion: Assuming the funds will be withdrawn during retirement and are invested in the same asset, $1 of pre-tax funds in a tax-deferred account such as a 401(k) will buy the same amount of goods and services as $(1 - t_n)$ dollar of after-tax funds in a tax-exempt account such as a Roth IRA, where t_n is the marginal tax rate in retirement. Tax-deferred account refers to a 401(k), 403(b), Keogh, SEP-IRA, or any other savings vehicle that contains pre-tax funds that are fully taxable at withdrawal as ordinary income. Because tax-deferred accounts and tax-exempt accounts look similar, to avoid confusion in this book, we will refer to tax-exempt accounts as tax-exempt Roths or, more simply, Roths. Roths include Roth IRAs, Roth 401(k)s, and Roth 403(b)s. *Since $1 of pre-tax funds in a tax-deferred account will buy the same amount of goods and services as $(1 - t_n)$ dollar of after-tax funds in a Roth, they should be considered equivalent today.*

Conceptually, *it is useful to separate each pre-tax dollar in a tax-deferred account into* $(1 - t_n)$ *dollar of the individual's after-tax funds plus* t_n *dollar, which is the government's share of the current principal.* In the example, Peggy, at age 50, has $10,000 of pre-tax funds in her 401(k). It is useful to think of this $10,000 as $7,500 of her after-tax funds plus $2,500, which is the government's share of the current principal. It is as if the government is a silent, limited partner in the tax-deferred account. The general partner—Peggy—gets to decide where the funds are invested. But whenever funds are withdrawn, the government will get t_n of the amount withdrawn. The government is effectively a limited partner, owning t_n of the current principal.[1]

The example is consistent with this analogy. The $10,000 of pre-tax funds in the 401(k) is essentially $7,500 of Peggy's after-tax funds, and the purchasing power of this $7,500 of after-tax funds is the same as the purchasing power of $7,500 of after-tax funds in the Roth IRA. Assuming the funds will be withdrawn during retirement—which is the usual assumption—the effective tax rate is t_n, the expected marginal tax rate during retirement.

RATIONALE OF AFTER-TAX ASSET ALLOCATION

Let us return to Peggy's situation at age 50. She has $10,000 of pre-tax funds in a 401(k) and $7,500 of after-tax funds in a Roth IRA. Suppose the 401(k) is invested in bonds and the Roth IRA is invested in stocks. If these are her only two assets, what is her asset allocation?

The after-tax approach to calculating an asset allocation first converts all market values to after-tax funds, and it then calculates the asset allocation based on after-tax balances. The $10,000 of pre-tax funds in the 401(k) is worth $7,500 after taxes or $10,000 $(1 - t_n)$. This after-tax approach says she has $7,500 of *after-tax* funds in bonds in the 401(k) and $7,500 of *after-tax* funds in stocks for an *after-tax asset allocation* of 50 percent bonds and 50 percent stocks.

In contrast, the traditional approach to calculating an asset allocation says Peggy has $10,000 in bonds and $7,500 in stocks for a 57 percent bonds and 43 percent stocks asset mix.

We believe the after-tax approach is the better approach to calculating an individual's asset allocation. Although this approach is more complex than the traditional approach, the reality is that taxes exist. Taxes matter! Unfortunately, the traditional approach fails to distinguish between pre-tax and after-tax funds. As this example illustrates, the traditional approach's measurement error can be substantial.

But We Don't Know t_n! To calculate Peggy's after-tax asset allocation, we must estimate t_n, the retirement tax rate. Peggy does not know what her tax rate will be in retirement. Moreover, the tax rate may vary from year to year during her retirement. To understand why it is better to calculate an after-tax asset allocation despite the need to estimate t_n, let's return to the example where she has $10,000 in bonds in the 401(k) and $7,500 in stocks in the Roth IRA.

The traditional approach says she has $10,000 in bonds and $7,500 in stocks, while the after-tax approach says she has $7,500 of after-tax funds in both bonds and stocks. The seeming advantage of the traditional approach is that it is based on certain values, while the after-tax approach requires an estimate of t_n. But the reality is that we are certain that withdrawals from the 401(k) will be subject to ordinary income taxes. The only uncertainty is the tax rate. Since the traditional approach fails to distinguish between pre-tax and after-tax funds it implicitly assumes her retirement tax rate will be zero. Although Peggy may not know what her retirement tax rate will be, it should be easy for her to improve upon the traditional approach's implicit estimate of zero. When calculating her asset allocation, it is better to estimate t_n and calculate an asset allocation that is approximately correct than one that is precisely wrong.

Let's review this important point again. The traditional approach fails to distinguish between pre-tax and after-tax funds. So, it implicitly assumes Peggy's retirement tax rate will be 0 percent. In this case, her asset allocation would be $10,000 of after-tax funds in bonds and $7,500 of after-tax funds in stocks. The traditional approach only accurately reflects Peggy's true asset allocation if she will be in the 0 percent tax bracket in retirement. Generalizing, *the traditional approach only accurately reflects individuals' asset allocations if taxes do not exist.* Although the calculation of an after-tax asset allocation is more complex, it is the better method because 1) it reflects the reality that taxes exist and 2) it compares after-tax funds in one savings vehicle to after-tax funds in other savings vehicles.

It should be noted that the recommendation to use an estimate—in this case of the expected tax rate in retirement—to calculate an asset's current value is not unique in the finance profession. Before the profession estimates the yield on a mortgage-backed security (MBS), it estimates the prepayment rate on the pool of mortgages. We know that few individuals will repay a 30-year mortgage over 30 years. Therefore, the profession recognizes that it is better to estimate the prepayment rate than to implicitly assume that no prepayments will occur. Given the estimated prepayment rate, the MBS's cash flows, average life, and yield can be estimated. What I recommend is for the finance profession to use the same idea when valuing pre-tax funds in tax-deferred accounts. Just as it is better to estimate mortgage prepayment rates than to assume prepayments will be zero, it is better to estimate the expected tax rate in retirement than to implicitly assume it will be zero.

The next chapter examines how the choice of savings vehicles—for example, taxable account, tax-deferred account, or Roth—affects the percent of principal effectively owned by, the percent of returns received by, and the percent of risk borne by individual investors. As we shall see, it supports the position that $1 of pre-tax funds in a tax-deferred account should be considered $(1 - t_n)$ dollar of after-tax funds in a Roth.

SUMMARY

Each dollar in a tax-deferred account is like $(1 - t_n)$ dollar in a tax-exempt Roth, where t_n is the marginal tax rate when the funds are withdrawn. It is useful to separate each pre-tax dollar in a tax-deferred account into $(1 - t_n)$ dollar of the individual's after-tax funds plus t_n, which is the government's share of the current principal. It is as if the government is a silent, limited partner in the tax deferred account. The after-tax asset allocation reflects the reality that taxes exist. In contrast, the traditional asset allocation ignores taxes and thus implicitly assumes that either taxes do not exist or the individual's tax rate will be zero. Although the calculation of an after-tax asset allocation is more complex, it is a better method of calculating an individual's asset allocation because 1) it reflects the reality that taxes exist and 2) it compares after-tax funds in one savings vehicle to after-tax funds in other savings vehicles.

In this chapter, we established the following principles and investment implications:

- Each dollar of *pre-tax* funds in a tax-deferred account is like $(1 - t_n)$ dollar of *after-tax* funds in a tax-exempt Roth, where t_n is the marginal tax rate when the funds are withdrawn.
- For each dollar of pre-tax funds in a tax-deferred account, the individual investor effectively owns $(1 - t_n)$ of the principal, while the government effectively owns the other t_n of current principal.
- The traditional approach to calculating an asset allocation fails to distinguish between before tax and after-tax funds. Stated differently, it implicitly assumes taxes do not exist.
- Although it is more complex to calculate an individual's after-tax asset allocation than her traditional asset allocation, it better measures her allocation because it recognizes that taxes exist and it compares after-tax funds in one savings vehicle to after-tax funds in other savings vehicles.

ENDNOTE
[1] I thank Jeffrey Horvitz for this analogy.

2 | *Principal, Risk, and Returns Sharing across Savings Vehicles*

This chapter shows how the choice of savings vehicles affects the percent of principal effectively owned by, the percent of return received by, and the percent of risk borne by individual investors. Related topics discussed in this chapter include the benefits of tax-deferred growth and tax-efficient management of stocks held in taxable accounts.

PRINCIPAL, RISK, AND RETURNS SHARING

Table 2.1 considers two asset classes—bonds and stocks—and four savings vehicles—tax-exempt Roth, tax-deferred account, taxable account, and non-qualified annuity. For each savings vehicle, the investor begins with $1 market value and we calculate its current and future after-tax values. The annual pre-tax rate of return is r, the investment horizon is n years, the ordinary income tax rate is t in years before withdrawal and t_n in the withdrawal year n years hence, and the tax rate on long-term capital gains and qualified dividends is t_c in all years.

Table 2.1. Prinicipal Owned, Returns Received, and Risk Borne by Individual Investors in Tax-exempt Roths, Tax-deferred Accounts, Taxable Accounts, and Non-qualified Annuities

	Principal	Returns	Risk
Tax-exempt Roths			
bonds and stocks	100%	100%	100%
Tax-deferred Accounts			
bonds and stocks	$(1 - t_n)$	100%	100%
Taxable Accounts			
bonds	100%	$(1 - t)$	$(1 - t)$
stocks, trader	100%	$(1 - t)$	$(1 - t)$
stocks, active investor	100%	$(1 - t_c)$	$(1 - t_c)$
stocks, passive investor	100%	$\geq (1 - t_c)$	$\geq (1 - t_c)$
stocks, exempt investor	100%	100%	100%
Non-qualified Annuities			
bonds and stocks	100%	$\geq (1 - t_n)$	$\geq (1 - t_n)$

The ordinary income tax rate is t in years before withdrawal and t_n in the withdrawal year, and the tax rate on long-term capital gains and qualified dividends is t_c in all years. Tax-exempt Roths include Roth IRAs, while tax-deferred accounts include 401(k)s, 403(b)s, Keoghs, and SEP-IRAs. Source: Adapted from Reichenstein (2007b)

Tax-exempt Roth. The $1 market value in a Roth account represents $1 of after-tax funds. For bonds and stocks, its after-tax value grows from $1 today to $(1 + r)^n$ dollars n years hence. This is the equation for compound return. If the annual return was 8 percent, then the future value of an original $1 investment in 20 years would be $4.66 or $(1.08)^{20}$.[1] This investor owns all principal, receives all returns, and bears all risk.

Tax-deferred Account. The $1 market value in a tax-deferred account represents $1 of pre-tax funds. For bonds and stocks, its after-tax value grows from $(1 - t_n)$ dollar today to $(1 + r)^n (1 - t_n)$ dollars n years hence. For a 25 percent tax rate in retirement, $t_n = 0.25$, the after-tax value of the dollar of pre-tax funds grows from $0.75 today to $0.75 $(1 + r)^n$ in n years. Since we assume the funds will be withdrawn during retirement, the effective tax rate is t_n, the expected tax rate in retirement, and not today's tax rate. The investor effectively owns $(1 - t_n)$ of principal, but receives all returns and bears all risk. As explained in Chapter 1, the tax-deferred account is like a trust, where the government is a silent partner that owns t_n of the trust and thus t_n of the current principal. This supports the conclusion from Chapter 1 that $1 of pre-tax funds in a tax-deferred account is like $(1 - t_n)$ dollar of after-tax funds in a tax-exempt Roth.

Bonds in Taxable Account. In this chapter, we assume the taxable account begins with $1 of after-tax funds, that is, the asset's cost basis equals its market value. (Chapter 3 considers situations where the cost basis and market value are not equal.) For bonds, the after-tax value grows from $1 today to $(1 + r(1 - t))^n$ dollars n years hence. The after-tax value grows at $r(1 - t)$. The investor owns all principal, but receives $(1 - t)$ of returns and bears $(1 - t)$ of risk.

To demonstrate the risk and returns sharing, assume bonds have a 4 percent expected return with a standard deviation of 6 percent. The ordinary income tax rate is 25 percent. For a three-year period, pre-tax returns are −2 percent, 4 percent, and 10 percent, that is, the 4 percent mean return and one standard deviation below and above the mean. The standard deviation of these returns is 6 percent. Assuming the 2 percent loss is used to offset that year's taxable income or short-term gains, the after-tax returns are −1.5 percent, 3 percent, and 7.5 percent. The mean after-tax return is 3 percent or $[4\%(1 - 0.25)]$, while the standard deviation is 4.5 percent or $[6\%(1 - 0.25)]$. In this case, the investor receives 75 percent of returns and bears 75 percent of the risk. If the 2 percent loss is used to offset that year's long-term gains, then the after-tax returns would be −1.7 percent, 3 percent, and 7.5 percent, and the

investor would receive approximately 75 percent of returns and
bears approximately 75 percent of risk. Although the investor with
bonds held in a taxable account may not receive precisely $(1 - t)$ of
return and bear precisely $(1 - t)$ of risk, Table 2.1 adopts this close
approximation. It assumes the investor receives $(1 - t)$ of pre-tax
returns and bears $(1 - t)$ of pre-tax risk.

Stocks in Taxable Accounts. For stocks held in taxable
accounts, the portion of returns received by and risk borne by the
individual investor varies with the stock management style. In this
section, we model individuals with four stock management styles.
The pre-tax return, r, is the sum of capital gain, g, and qualifying
dividend yield, d; that is, $r = g + d$.

The trader realizes all gains within one year and pays taxes
at the ordinary income tax rate. His after-tax value grows from
$1 today to $(1 + g(1 - t) + d(1 - t_c))^n$ dollars n years hence.
Assume capital gains average 6 percent and dividend yield
averages 2 percent for the long horizons associated with most
retirement savings. In this case, the trader owns all principal,
but receives 78 percent or $[\{6\%(0.75) + 2\%(0.85)\}/8\%]$ of
returns, and bears about 78 percent of risk.[2] After 2010, dividends are scheduled to be taxed as ordinary income again. At
that time, the trader would own all principal, but receive 75
percent or $[\{6\%(0.75) + 2\%(0.75)\}/8\%]$ of returns and bear
75 percent of risk. Table 2.1 assumes this trader receives $(1 - t)$
of returns and bears $(1 - t)$ of risk.

The active investor realizes all gains in one year and one day and
pays taxes at t_c on capital gains and qualifying dividends. The active
investor holds stocks just long enough to qualify for the preferential
long-term gain tax rate, t_c, but he or she does not allow the gains to
grow unharvested and thus benefit from tax-deferred growth. The
after-tax value grows from $1 today to $(1 + r(1 - t_c))^n$ dollars n years
hence. This investor owns all principal, but receives $(1 - t_c)$ of returns
and bears $(1 - t_c)$ of risk.

To demonstrate the risk and returns sharing, assume stocks have an 8 percent expected return with a standard deviation of 15 percent. The dividend and capital gain tax rates are 15 percent. For a three-year period, pre-tax stock returns are −7 percent, 8 percent, and 23 percent, that is, the 8 percent mean return and one standard deviation below and above the mean. The standard deviation of these returns is 15 percent. Assuming the 7 percent loss is used to offset long-term gains, the active investor's after-tax returns are −5.95 percent, 6.8 percent, and 19.55 percent. In this case, the mean after-tax return is 6.8 percent or $[8\%(1 - 0.15)]$, while the after-tax standard deviation is 12.75 percent or $[15\%(1 - 0.15)]$. The investor receives 85 percent of returns and bears 85 percent of risk; the government receives 15 percent of returns and bears 15 percent of risk. If the 7 percent loss is used to offset this year's taxable income or short-term gains, then the active investor receives approximately 85 percent of returns and bears approximately 85 percent of risk. Table 2.1 assumes the active investor receives $(1 - t_c)$ of returns and bears $(1 - t_c)$ of risk.

The passive investor benefits from tax-deferred growth. Since this benefit is examined in detail later in this chapter, we defer discussion of the passive stock investor until then.

The exempt investor never realizes gains and never pays taxes on the gains, but he or she pays taxes each year on dividends. Eventually, the appreciated stock is either donated to charity or sold after receiving the step-up in basis. If donated to a qualifying charity, the individual can deduct the stock's market value and the charity can sell the stock without incurring taxes. At the death of the individual, the stock's cost basis increases to the market value at death, so the beneficiary can sell it without incurring capital gain taxes. The after-tax value grows from \$1 today to $(1 + g + d(1 - t_c))^n$ dollars n years hence. This investor owns all principal. For most stocks, he receives almost all returns and bears all risk. For example, if the dividend yield is 2 percent and capital gains average 6 percent then, on average, the investor receives 96.3 percent or [{6% + 2%(1 – 0.15)}/8%] of returns and bears almost all risk.[3]

BENEFITS OF TAX-DEFERRED GROWTH

We now illustrate the advantages of tax-deferred growth. It applies to 1) passively-managed stock held in a taxable account and 2) bonds or stocks held in a non-qualified annuity.

Passively-managed Stocks. Since this section is concerned about the benefits of tax-deferred growth, let's assume all of the passively-managed stocks' returns are in the form of capital gains; that is, there are no dividends. The after-tax value grows from $1 today to the following values after withdrawal in n years:

$$(1 + r)^n - t_c[(1 + r)^n - 1] \text{ or} \qquad (2.1a)$$
$$(1 + r)^n (1 - t_c) + t_c \qquad (2.1b)$$

Equation 2.1a can be interpreted as follows. The original $1 grows to $(1 + r)^n$ dollars after n years. At withdrawal, taxes at t_c, the long-term capital gain tax rate, are due on deferred returns, where the amount in brackets, $[(1 + r)^n - 1]$, represents deferred returns. For example, suppose the original $1 grows at 7 percent per year for 20 years and is worth $3.87. The $3.87 is withdrawn, and taxes are due at t_c on the $2.87 of tax-deferred returns. The original $1 was already after-tax funds, so it can be withdrawn tax free.

Equation 2.1b, which is algebraically equivalent to Equation 2.1a, can be explained as follows. At withdrawal, the entire withdrawal amount, $(1 + r)^n$, is taxed at t_c, but then the investor receives an additional t_c (times the cost basis of $1), which is the taxes saved because the original $1 can be withdrawn tax free. From the prior example, the $3.87 is taxed at t_c, but then we add $0.15 to $(1 + r)^n (1 - t_c)$, because the $1 original principal can be withdrawn tax free.

Table 2.2. Effective Tax Rates by Investment Horizon for 8 Percent Return			
Investment Horizon (Years)	**Eventual Tax Rate**		
	15%	**25%**	**35%**
1	15%	25%	35%
3	14.1%	23.6%	33.3%
5	13.2%	22.3%	31.6%
10	11.3%	19.3%	27.8%
15	9.7%	16.8%	24.4%
20	8.4%	14.7%	21.5%
25	7.4%	12.9%	19%
30	6.5%	11.4%	16.9%
35	5.8%	10.2%	15.2%
40	5.2%	9.2 %	13.6%

The effective tax rate is tax rate that would produce the same after-tax ending wealth if all returns were taxed annually at this rate. For example, for a three-year horizon and 15 percent eventual tax rate, $(1 + 0.08(1 - 0.141))^3 = (1.08)^3 (1 - 0.15) + 0.15$.

The second column of Table 2.2 illustrates the advantages of tax-deferred growth for a passive stock investor. For an 8 percent annual tax-deferred return, it presents the effective tax rates for a passive stock investor who holds the stock until the end of the investment horizon, at which time taxes are paid on the deferred returns at 15 percent. There is little benefit to deferring gains for a few years. For example, for a three-year horizon, the effective tax rate is 14.1 percent, less than 1 percent lower than the long-term capital gain rate. The 14.1 percent effective rate means that the after-tax wealth after three years is the same as if the return was fully taxed each year at 14.1 percent.[4] The effective tax rate decreases as the horizon lengthens. For 10 and 20 year horizons, the effective tax rates are 11.3 percent and 8.4 percent. The 8.4 percent is more than 40 percent lower than the 15 percent rate, which indicates the substantial advantage to tax-deferred growth for long investment horizons.

Non-qualified Annuity. In this chapter, we assume the $1 market value in the non-qualified annuity is $1 of after-tax funds. That is, the individual invests $1 today in a non-qualified annuity. The term "non-qualified" means that the investment amount does not qualify for tax deduction this year; thus the initial investment consists of $1 of after-tax funds. (Chapter 3 considers situations where an annuity's market value consists of a combination of after-tax and pre-tax funds.) Returns grow tax deferred until withdrawal, at which time taxes are due on the deferred returns.

For bonds and stocks held in a non-qualified annuity, the after-tax value grows from $1 today to the following value n years hence:

$$(1 + r)^n - t_n[(1 + r)^n - 1] \text{ or} \qquad (2.2a)$$
$$(1 + r)^n (1 - t_n) + t_n \qquad (2.2b)$$

Equations 2.2a and 2.2b are the same as Equations 2.1a and 2.1b, except the applicable tax rate is t_n, the ordinary income tax rate. Even if the underlying asset's return is in the form of capital gains or dividends, they are eventually taxed at the ordinary income tax rate. Equations 2.2a and 2.2b are conceptually equivalent to Equations 2.1a and 2.1b. For example, $(1 + r)^n (1 - t_n) + t_n$ says its ending after-tax wealth is as if the full withdrawal were taxed at t_n, but the investor receives an additional t_n (times the $1 cost basis) since the original $1 can be withdrawn tax free.

Equations 2.2a and 2.2b also reflect the tax structure facing non-deductible contributions to traditional IRAs and investments in U.S. savings bonds. These contributions or original investment amounts are made with after-tax funds, but returns grow tax deferred until withdrawal, at which time tax-deferred returns are taxed as ordinary income. Furthermore, although these equations reflect the tax structure facing non-qualified annuities, they ignore some annuity features.[5]

The last two columns of Table 2.2 present the effective tax rates for a non-qualified annuity with an 8 percent return when the deferred returns are eventually taxed at 25 percent and 35 percent, respectively. For the 25 percent tax rate, the effective rates are 23.6 percent after 3 years, 19.3 percent after 10 years, and 14.7 percent after 20 years. For the 35 percent tax rate, the effective rates are 33.3 percent after 3 years, 27.8 percent after 10 years, and 21.5 percent after 20 years. Although terms such as "large" and "small" are always open to interpretation, the numbers suggest that the benefits of tax deferral are small for short horizons (for example, five years or less) but large for horizons of ten years or longer.

COMPARISON OF EFFECTIVE TAX RATES ACROSS SAVINGS VEHICLES

Table 2.3 compares the effective tax rates for investments in tax-exempt Roths, tax-deferred accounts, taxable accounts, and non-qualified annuities. For bonds and stocks held in Roths or tax-deferred accounts, the effective tax rate is zero. For bonds held in taxable accounts, the effective tax rate is t, the ordinary income tax rate, while for stocks, the effective tax rate is substantially above zero except for the exempt investor. Returns on bonds and stocks held in a non-qualified annuity grow tax deferred, but as Table 2.2 demonstrates, there is a big difference between *tax-exempt* growth and *tax-deferred* growth. In short, with the exception of stocks held in taxable accounts by an exempt investor when saving for retirement, the effective tax rates on tax-deferred accounts and Roths are much lower than the effective tax rates in the other savings vehicles. Therefore, in general, when saving for retirement, individuals should save all they are allowed to save or all they can afford to save in tax-deferred accounts and Roths. Chapter 4 examines in greater depth the choice of savings vehicles when saving for retirement. After exhausting savings opportunities in these most tax-favored savings vehicles, if they want to save additional amounts for retirement, they should consider the merits of saving in a taxable account versus a non-qualified annuity.

Table 2.3. Effective Tax Rates Assuming 25 Percent Ordinary Income Tax Rate and 15 Percent Capital Gain Tax Rate	
	Effective Tax Rates
Tax-exempt Roths	
bonds and stocks	0%
Tax-deferred Accounts	
bonds and stocks	0%
Taxable Accounts	
bonds	25%
stocks, trader	≈25%
stocks, active investor	15%
stocks, passive investor	≤15%
stocks, exempt investor	≈0%
Non-qualified Annuities	
bonds and stocks	≤25%

The ordinary income tax rate is 25 percent and the tax rate on long-term capital gains and qualified dividends is 15 percent. Tax-exempt Roths include Roth IRAs, while tax-deferred accounts include 401(k)s, 403(b)s, Keoghs, and SEP-IRAs.

TAX-EFFICIENT STOCK MANAGEMENT

Most of the tax-efficient investment literature deals with the tax-efficient management of stocks held in taxable accounts. For example, see Jeffrey and Arnott (1993). As just discussed, for most individual investors, tax-efficient stock management requires maximizing contributions to Roths and tax-deferred accounts. After all, a zero percent effective tax rate on Roths and tax-deferred accounts beats the positive effective tax rates paid by a trader, active investor, and passive stock investor. The tax-efficient stock management literature emphasizes two principles. First, in general, individual investors should delay recognition of capital gains for as long as possible and, second, they should aggressively realize capital losses that are large enough to offset transaction costs.

The four hypothetical stock investors illustrate the first principle. The trader pays an effective tax rate on capital gains of t, the ordinary income tax rate. By realizing the gains after a year and a day, the effective tax rate for the active investor is reduced to t_c, the long-term capital gain tax rate. Unless an individual has offsetting capital losses, he should seldom realize a short-term gain. Compared to the active investor, the passive investor receives the benefits of tax-deferred growth, which lowers the effective tax rate below t_c. However, the effective tax rate is not substantially lower unless the investment horizon is ten years or longer. Compared to the passive investor, the exempt investor avoids taxes on capital gains by either awaiting the step-up in basis at death or by donating the appreciated asset to a qualified charity. Again, in general, it pays to delay recognition of gains for as long as possible.

The other principle of tax-efficient stock management is to aggressively realize capital losses. Capital losses can be used to offset capital gains and reduce taxable income. In either case, the government shares in the realized losses by lowering the individual's taxes. Most of the tax-efficient stock management literature deals with applications of these two principles.

Chapter 1 introduced the concept that each dollar in a tax-deferred account should be considered the equivalent of $(1 - t_n)$ dollar in a Roth. This chapter further developed this concept. The next chapter applies this insight by recommending that an individual calculate his or her after-tax asset allocation. In addition, it addresses other issues related to the calculation of after-tax asset allocation, including the treatment of unrealized capital gains and losses on assets held in taxable accounts.

SUMMARY
Table 2.1 summarizes this chapter. For bonds and stocks held in a tax-exempt Roth, the investor owns all principal, receives all

returns, and bears all risk. For bonds and stocks held in a tax-deferred account, he owns $(1 - t_n)$ of principal, but receives all returns and bears all risk. For bonds held in a taxable account (with market value equal to cost basis), the investor owns all principal, but receives approximately $(1 - t)$ of returns and bears approximately $(1 - t)$ of risk. For stocks held in taxable accounts (with market value equal to cost basis), the investor owns all principal, but the portion of returns received by and risk borne by the individual varies with the stock management style. For the trader, the portion is approximately $(1 - t)$; for the active investor, it is approximately $(1 - t_c)$; for the passive investor with a multiyear investment horizon, it exceeds $(1 - t_c)$; and for the exempt investor, it is approximately 100 percent. In a non-qualified annuity (with market value equal to cost basis), the investor owns all principal, but for a multiyear horizon, he receives more than $(1 - t_n)$ of returns and bears more than $(1 - t_n)$ of risk.

In this chapter, we established the following principles and investment implications:

- For bonds and stocks held in a tax-exempt Roth, the investor owns all principal, receives all returns, and bears all risk.
- For bonds and stocks held in a tax-deferred account, he owns $(1 - t_n)$ of principal, but receives all returns and bears all risk, where t_n is the ordinary income tax rate in retirement.
- For bonds held in a taxable account (with market value equal to cost basis), the investor owns all principal, but receives approximately $(1 - t)$ of returns and bears approximately $(1 - t)$ of risk, where t is the ordinary income tax rate.
- For stocks held in taxable accounts (with market value equal to cost basis), the investor owns all principal, but the portion of returns received by and risk borne by the individual varies with the stock management style. For the trader, the portion is approximately $(1 - t)$; for the active investor, it is approximately

$(1 - t_c)$, where t_c is the long-term capital gain tax rate; for the passive investor with a multiyear investment horizon, it exceeds $(1 - t_c)$; and for the exempt investor, it is approximately 100 percent.

- In a non-qualified annuity (with market value equal to cost basis), the investor owns all principal, but for a multiyear horizon he receives more than $(1 - t_n)$ of returns and bears more than $(1 - t_n)$ of risk.
- Stated differently, the effective tax rate is 0 percent on bonds and stocks held in Roths or tax-deferred accounts, t on bonds held in taxable accounts, about t_c on stocks held in taxable accounts by an active investor, and less than t_n on bonds and stocks held for a multiyear horizon in a non-qualified annuity.
- In general, when saving for retirement, individuals should save all they are allowed to save or all they can afford to save in tax-deferred accounts and Roths.

ENDNOTES

[1] In a financial calculator, PV = $1, PMT = 0, i = 8, n = 20, and FV = $4.66.

[2] The trader receives 75 percent of the 6 percent capital gain plus 85 percent of the 2 percent dividend yield for an after-tax return of 6.2 percent. So, the trader receives 6.2/8 or about 78 percent of the 8 percent pre-tax return.

[3] If the dividend yield is constant, then the volatility in annual return is due entirely to the capital gain. In this case, the volatility of after-tax returns is due entirely to the capital gain portion of return, and the exempt investor bears all risk. Even if the dividend yield varies, it should be clear that the exempt investor bears almost all risk.

[4] Mathematically, $(1 + 0.08(1 - 0.141))^3 = (1.08)^3(1 - 0.15) + 0.15$.

[5] For example, Equations 2.2a and 2.2b ignore the surrender fees and death benefit typically found in annuities. Most annuities impose surrender fees that may be 7 percent of withdrawals in the first contract year, with the penalty decreasing 1 percent per year thereafter and disappearing after seven years. In addition, most annuities charge about 1.25 percent higher annual expense ratios than would exist on a similar bond or stock investment held in a taxable account. These higher fees affect the investor's net returns, and should influence the decision to invest in a non-qualified annuity or another savings vehicle. Annuities usually offer a death benefit. A typical death benefit guarantees that, at death, the beneficiary will receive the larger of the then-current account value or the

original investment (less prior withdrawals). This death benefit partially offsets the higher fees. For more on the merits of annuities as vehicles for accumulating retirement wealth, see Reichenstein (2003b) and Reichenstein and Jennings (2003). For a discussion of the merits of annuities as a vehicle for distributing retirement wealth, see Reichenstein (2003a).

3

How to Calculate an After-tax Asset Allocation

To calculate an after-tax asset allocation, we first convert all assets' market values to after-tax values and then calculate the asset allocation using these after-tax values. Chapter 1 explained the rationale of calculating an after-tax asset allocation. The traditional approach fails to distinguish between pre- and after-tax funds. In contrast, the after-tax approach adjusts assets' market values for embedded tax liabilities. As such, it compares after-tax dollars in one savings vehicle to after-tax dollars in other savings vehicles.

The disadvantage of the after-tax approach is that it is more complex than the traditional approach. For example, to adjust for the embedded tax liability in tax-deferred accounts, we must estimate t_n, the tax rate during retirement. However, taxes exist, and to accurately measure an individual's true asset allocation, we must face the reality that withdrawals from tax-deferred accounts will be subject to taxes. As noted in Chapter 1, the traditional approach ignores taxes and thus implicitly assumes the tax rate in retirement will be zero. Although we may be uncertain about what an individual's retirement tax rate will be, it is usually easy to improve on the implicit assumption of zero. When calculating an individual's asset allocation, it is better to estimate the retirement tax rate than to ignore taxes.

In this chapter, we will discuss other assumptions that sometimes have to be made to convert assets' market values to after-tax values. However, the same principle applies: It is better to face the reality that taxes exist and to make reasonable adjustments for taxes than to ignore them. Therefore, the after-tax approach to calculating an asset allocation should provide a better measure of an individual's asset allocation than the traditional approach.

Finally, it is important to note that the finance profession routinely uses estimates when valuing mortgage-backed securities. So, what we are proposing here is not unique. Few individuals repay a 30-year mortgage over 30 years. Consequently, the profession has long recognized that it is better to estimate prepayment rates and calculate an MBS's cash flows, average life, and yield that are approximately right than to assume that there will be no prepayments and calculate cash flows, average life, and yield that are precisely wrong. The same analogy applies here. The finance profession should recognize that it is better to estimate the tax rate in retirement and calculate an individual's asset allocation that is approximately correct than to assume no taxes and calculate an asset allocation that is precisely wrong.

CONVERSION TO AFTER-TAX VALUES

The first step in calculating an after-tax asset allocation is to convert assets' market values to after-tax values. Stated differently, we need to adjust assets' market values for embedded tax liabilities. In this section, we discuss the Reichenstein and Jennings approach to making these adjustments for funds held in tax-exempt Roths, tax-deferred accounts, taxable accounts, and non-qualified annuities (see Reichenstein, 2006a and 2007a, and Reichenstein and Jennings, 2003).

Tax-exempt Roths. Withdrawals from a Roth are tax exempt provided that the account has been in existence for at least five years and the individual is at least 59.5. We assume the provisional conditions prevail. Therefore, there is no need to adjust the market values of a Roth for taxes. Each $1 in a Roth is worth $1 of after-tax funds.

Tax-deferred Accounts. Withdrawals from a tax-deferred account are taxable as ordinary income. With some exceptions, withdrawals before the age of 59.5 are subject to an additional 10 percent penalty tax. But we assume withdrawals will occur after 59.5. To convert pre-tax funds in a tax-deferred account to after-tax values, we multiply by the percentage $(1 - t_n)$, where t_n is the expected tax rate in retirement.

As explained in Chapters 1 and 2, each $1 in a tax-deferred account is like $(1 - t_n)$ dollar in a Roth, where t_n is the expected ordinary income tax rate during retirement. If invested in the same asset, $1 in a tax-deferred account will buy the same amount of goods and services as $(1 - t_n)$ dollar in a Roth. When calculating an asset allocation, we should treat $1 of pre-tax funds in a tax-deferred account as if it is $(1 - t_n)$ dollar of after-tax funds in a Roth. Conceptually, it is useful to separate each dollar in a tax-deferred account into two parts: $(1 - t_n)$ dollar of the individual's after-tax funds plus t_n dollar, which is the government's share of the current principal. For example, someone who expects to be in the 25 percent tax bracket in retirement should consider $100,000 in bonds in a 401(k) as $75,000 of her after-tax funds in bonds.

Taxable Accounts. If the market value and cost basis of an asset held in a taxable account are the same, then the asset's after-tax value is its market value; there is no need to adjust the market value for taxes. Even if an asset's market value and cost basis differ, there may be no need to adjust the market value.

For example, suppose someone bought a bond at issue for $1,000, and he expects to hold the bond until maturity. If interest rates have fallen since issue, the bond will be selling at a premium to par, but if rates have risen since issue, the bond will be selling at a discount to par. However, if he holds the bond until maturity, there will be no tax consequences from these embedded gains and losses. So, the after-tax value is the market value.

Suppose, instead, that this individual has assets held in a taxable account that have embedded but unrealized capital gains or losses and he expects to realize the gains or losses in a taxable transaction. In these cases, it would be appropriate to reduce the asset's market value for the tax liability of the embedded gain or increase the market value for the tax savings from the embedded loss. Examples will illustrate this idea.

Let's first discuss capital losses. Suppose Peggy owns a stock with a market value of $20,000 and cost basis of $25,000. Further assume she is in the 25 percent ordinary income tax bracket and 15 percent capital gain tax bracket and will remain in these brackets. This example and the ones to follow assume the asset is a stock, but it could be any capital asset. If she will realize the loss, then the tax consequences of that loss should be considered in today's after-tax value. If she realizes the loss today, it would be used first to offset capital gains and second to reduce taxable income up to $3,000 per year. If the loss would be used this year to offset $5,000 of long-term capital gains, then the tax savings would be $750 or [$5,000(0.15)], and the asset's after-tax value would be $20,750. If the loss is used this year to offset $2,000 of long-term gains and $3,000 of taxable income, then the tax savings would be $300 from the capital gain offset and $750 from the income reduction. The after-tax value would be $21,050.

Suppose she has a stock with a market value of $20,000 and cost basis of $16,000. Let's consider the valuation implications of the embedded gains for individuals with the four stock management styles discussed in Chapter 2.

If she is a trader, she will realize the gain as a short-term capital gain this year. Since short-term gains are taxed as ordinary income, taxes on the $4,000 gain will be $1,000 and the after-tax value is $19,000.

If she is an active investor, she will realize the gain as a long-term gain this year. Taxes will be $600 and the after-tax value is $19,400.

If she is a passive investor, she will allow the gains to grow unrealized for years but eventually realize the gains. If the capital gain tax rate is 15 percent then she will eventually owe $600 in taxes on the gains. As discussed in Appendix C, the stock's after-tax value is $19,400, $20,000 market value less the $600 tax liability.

If she is an exempt investor then there will be no taxes on the embedded gains, and the after-tax value is $20,000, the same as the market value. The capital gains will be tax exempt under two scenarios: if she awaits the step-up in basis at death or uses the appreciated asset to finance a charitable donation.

In short, the after-tax value is the market value less the embedded tax liability. For the trader, the liability is $1,000. For the active and passive investors, it is $600. For the exempt investor, there is no tax liability. So, the "right" way to handle the tax consequences of the unrealized gain depends upon how quickly, if ever, she will realize the gain. A financial adviser can add value to clients' accounts by helping them understand the tax consequences of their actions.

Non-qualified Annuities. If the market value and cost basis of an asset held in a non-qualified annuity are the same, then the asset's after-tax value is its market value. If the market value exceeds the cost basis then we need to adjust the market value for the embedded tax liability on the deferred returns. In contrast, if the market value is less than the cost basis, we should not adjust the market value for the embedded capital loss because losses realized in a non-qualified account can seldom be used to reduce taxable income.[1]

As discussed in Appendix C, when the market value exceeds the cost basis, the after-tax value of an annuity is the market value less the tax liability as if the deferred returns were realized today and taxed at the ordinary income tax rate. Suppose the annuity has a market value of $15,000 and cost basis of $10,000. The after-tax value is $13,750, $15,000 less the tax liability of $1,250 on the $5,000 of deferred returns

Suppose the annuity has a market value of $9,000 and cost basis of $10,000. The after-tax value is $9,000 because the $1,000 loss, even if realized, can seldom be used to reduce taxable income. To be deductible, the $1,000 loss could be used as a miscellaneous itemized deduction to the degree it exceeds 2 percent of Adjusted Gross Income. So, if the investor itemizes and if her AGI is $45,000, then $100 would be tax deductible, where $100 is the amount of the loss in excess of 2 percent of AGI. In practice, investors seldom meet these dual criteria, and annuity losses are seldom deductible. In general, a realized loss can only be used to offset realized capital gains or to reduce income if the asset is held in a taxable account.

The after-tax value of an asset held in a tax-exempt Roth is the same as its market value. The after-tax value of an asset held in a tax-deferred account is its market value multiplied by $(1 - t_n)$. The after-tax value of an asset held in a taxable account is the market value less the tax liability associated with any unrealized gain or plus the tax savings associated with any unrealized capital loss. The after-tax value of a non-qualified annuity is its market value less the tax liability associated with any embedded tax-deferred returns. Appendixes A and C present some of the theoretical work related to calculating assets' after-tax values.

EXAMPLES
This section presents examples of the calculation of individuals' after-tax asset allocations.

Example 1. Table 3.1 presents Carla's portfolio. She expects to have a 25 percent ordinary income tax rate in retirement. She has $600,000 in bonds and $100,000 in stocks held in tax-deferred accounts, and $300,000 in stocks held in Roth IRAs. To calculate her after-tax asset allocation, we must first adjust funds in the tax-deferred account for taxes. The $600,000 of pre-tax funds in bonds in the tax-deferred accounts is worth $450,000 after taxes, [$600,000 (1 – 0.25)], while the $100,000 in stocks is worth $75,000 after taxes. The stocks held in the Roth IRAs are worth $300,000 after taxes; there is no adjustment for taxes. The after-tax asset allocation contains $450,000 in bonds and $375,000 in stocks for a 54.5 percent bonds/45.5 percent stocks asset mix.

Table 3.1. Example 1—Calculation of Carla's After-tax Asset Allocation

Asset Class	Market Values	After-tax Values	Savings Vehicle
Bonds	$600,000	$450,000	tax-deferred accounts
Stocks	$100,000	$75,000	tax-deferred accounts
Stocks	+$300,000	+$300,000	tax-exempt Roths
Total	$1,000,000	$825,000	

Carla expects to have a 25% ordinary income tax rate in retirement. Her after-tax asset allocation is 54.5% bonds/45.5% stocks, while the traditional approach says the allocation is 60% bonds/40% stocks.

In contrast, when calculated using the traditional approach, her portfolio contains $600,000 in bonds and $400,000 in stocks for a 60 percent bonds/40 percent stocks asset allocation. In this example, it overstates the bond allocation by 5.5 percent.

This example clearly illustrates the problem with the traditional approach. It ignores taxes and thus implicitly assumes that taxes do not exist. Whether this individual is wealthy or a pauper, the traditional approach would say her asset allocation is 60 percent bonds/40 percent stocks. The pauper's tax rate in retirement might be zero. So, in that case, the pre-tax and after-tax values of tax-deferred accounts would be the same. In the more general case, where t_n will be positive, the traditional approach fails to adjust for the embedded tax liability. Therefore, *the traditional approach exaggerates the allocation to the dominant asset held in tax-deferred accounts.*

Example 2. Table 3.2 presents Sam's portfolio. He is in the 15 percent capital gain tax bracket and expects to have a 25 percent ordinary income tax rate in retirement. He has $600,000 of bonds in tax-deferred accounts, $100,000 in stocks in Roth IRAs, and $300,000 in stocks in taxable accounts. The latter have a cost basis of $260,000. He will eventually realize the gain as a long-term gain.

To calculate his after-tax asset allocation, we must first convert all accounts to after-tax values. The $600,000 in tax-deferred accounts is worth $450,000 after taxes, [$600,000 (1 – 0.25)]. The stocks held in taxable accounts are worth $294,000 after taxes, $300,000 less $6,000 in taxes on the $40,000 of unrealized gains. The after-tax asset allocation contains $450,000 in bonds and $394,000 in stocks for a 53.3 percent bonds/46.7 percent stocks asset mix.

Table 3.2. Example 2—Calculation of Sam's After-tax Asset Allocation

Asset Class	Market Values	After-tax Values	Savings Vehicle
Bonds	$600,000	$450,000	tax-deferred accounts
Stocks	$100,000	$100,000	tax-deferred accounts
Stocks	+$300,000	$294,000	tax-exempt Roths
Total	$1,000,000	$844,000	

Sam expects to have a 25% ordinary income tax rate in retirement. He is in the 15% long-term capital gain tax bracket and expects to remain in this bracket. Cost basis of stocks in taxable account is $260,000. His after-tax asset allocation is 53.3% bonds/46.7% stocks, while the traditional approach says the allocation is 60% bonds/40% stocks.

In contrast, when calculated using the traditional approach, his portfolio contains $600,000 in bonds and $400,000 in stocks for a 60 percent bonds/40 percent stocks asset allocation. It overstates the bond allocation by 6.7 percent. Moreover, many U.S. investors, especially high net worth investors, tend to have higher ordinary income tax brackets. Many non-U.S. individuals face higher tax rates as well. For example, many Canadians face 40 percent or higher marginal tax brackets. If the tax rate was 40 percent in this example, the traditional approach would overstate the bond allocation by 12.3 percent. Neither the 6.7 percent nor the 12.3 percent measurement error is minor.

Example 3. Table 3.3 presents Maria's portfolio. She has a 15 percent capital gain tax rate and expects to have a 35 percent tax rate on ordinary income during retirement. She has $5 million of pre-tax funds in bonds in tax-deferred accounts and $500,000 in bonds in Roths. In taxable accounts, she has Stock Fund A, a passive stock fund that she bought years earlier. It has a market value of $250,000 and a cost basis of $100,000. She plans to donate these funds to a qualified charity. Stock Fund B has a market value of $3,250,000 and a cost basis of $3,050,000. She will eventually realize this gain and pay taxes at 15 percent. In addition, she has a non-qualified fixed annuity. She contributed $750,000 into this annuity years earlier, and its market value is $1 million. So, there is $250,000 in tax-deferred returns.

Table 3.3. Example 3—Calculation of Maria's After-tax Asset Allocation

Asset Class	Market Values	After-tax Values	Savings Vehicle
Bonds	$5,000,000	$3,250,000	tax-deferred accounts
Bonds	$500,000	$500,000	Roth IRAs
Bonds	$1,000,000	$912,500	non-qualified fixed annuities
Stock Fund A	$250,000	$250,000	taxable accounts
Stock Fund B	+$3,250,000	+$3,220,000	taxable accounts
Total	$10,000,000	$8,132,500	

Maria has a 15% long-term capital gain tax rate and expects to have a 35% ordinary income tax rate in retirement. Cost bases of Stock Funds A and B are $100,000 and $3,050,000, respectively. The individual intends to donate Stock Fund A to a qualified charity and expects to realize the gain in Stock Fund B. Her after-tax asset allocation is 57.3% bonds/42.7% stocks, while the traditional approach says the allocation is 65% bonds/35% stocks.

To calculate her after-tax asset allocation, we must first convert all accounts to after-tax values. The $5 million in the tax-deferred account is worth $3,250,000 after taxes, [$5,000,000(1 – 0.35)]. Stock Fund A is worth $250,000 after taxes. Although it has $150,000 in unrealized gains, she expects to donate this appreciated asset to a charity, and thus avoid taxes on these gains. Stock Fund B has a market value of $3,250,000 and cost basis of $3,050,000. The after-tax value is $3,220,000 or $3,250,000 less taxes at 15 percent on the $200,000 long-term gain. The $1 million annuity contains $750,000 of after-tax funds and $250,000 of pre-tax deferred returns. Its after-tax value is thus $912,500 or $1 million less the $87,500 tax liability on the $250,000 of deferred returns.

Table 3.3 presents these values. Her portfolio contains $4,662,500 of after-tax funds in bonds and $3,470,000 of after-tax funds in stocks for a 57.3 percent bonds/42.7 percent stocks mix. For comparison, the traditional approach says she has a 65 percent bonds/35 percent stocks mix. So, the traditional approach's measurement error is 7.7 percent. As before, the traditional approach exaggerates the allocation to the dominant asset held in tax-deferred accounts.

In my experience, the largest tax adjustment by far is usually the conversion of pre-tax funds in tax-deferred accounts to after-tax values. There is usually relatively little difference between market values and after-tax values of assets held in taxable accounts and non-qualified annuities. In Example 1, the only adjustment is to tax-deferred accounts. In Example 2, there was a $150,000 adjustment to tax-deferred accounts and only a $6,000 adjustment to taxable accounts. In Example 3, there was a $1,750,000 adjustment to tax-deferred accounts, $87,500 adjustment to the annuity, and $30,000 adjustment to the taxable accounts. To repeat, the largest adjustments were the need to convert the tax-deferred accounts' pre-tax funds to after-tax values.

Example 4. A client and her financial adviser determine that the client's risk tolerance is such that she should have an asset allocation of 40 percent bonds/60 percent stocks. Using the traditional approach, they put her in the portfolio in Table 3.4 that they believe meets the 40 percent/60 percent target mix. Moreover, based on projected stock returns of 10 percent and bond returns of 5 percent, the adviser told her the portfolio offers an 8 percent expected return, $[0.6(0.10) + 0.4(0.05)]$. The client expects to have a 25 percent ordinary income tax rate in retirement. She has a 15 percent capital gain tax rate and is an active stock investor. First, we calculate the client's after-tax asset allocation. Second, we calculate the after-tax rate of return based on the after-tax asset allocation.

From Table 3.4, the after-tax values of the bonds and stocks held in tax-deferred accounts are $300,000 and $150,000, while the stocks held in the taxable account have an after-tax value of $400,000. The after-tax asset allocation is 35.3 percent bonds/64.7 percent stocks or 4.7 percent above the target stock allocation. If the 40 percent/60 percent mix is optimal then the optimal allocation to stocks is $510,000 of after-tax funds, $[0.6(\$850,000)]$. So she needs to move $40,000 of after-tax funds ($53,333 or $[\$40,000/(1 - 0.25)]$ of pre-tax funds) from stocks to bonds in tax-deferred accounts. Although she could attain the 60 percent/40 percent target mix by moving $40,000 from stocks to bonds in taxable accounts, as we shall see in Chapter 5 the *asset-location* preference is to move the $40,000 of after-tax funds from tax-deferred accounts.

Table 3.4. Example 4—Calculation of an Individual's After-tax Asset Allocation

Asset Class	Market Values	After-tax Values	Savings Vehicle
Bonds	$400,000	$300,000	tax-deferred accounts
Bonds	$200,000	$150,000	tax-deferred account
Stocks	+$400,000	+$400,000	taxable account
Total	$1,000,000	$850,000	

The individual is in and expects to remain in the 25% ordinary income and 15% capital gain tax brackets. She is an active stock investor. Her target asset allocation is 40% bonds/60% stocks, and her portfolio is presented above. Cost basis of stocks in taxable account is $400,000. The after-tax asset allocation is 35.3% bonds/64.7% stocks, while the traditional approach says it is 40% bonds/60% stocks.

Separately, the after-tax rate of return of the after-tax portfolio is approximately 7.5 percent, which is calculated as follows:

($300,000/$850,000)(0.05) + ($150,000/$850,000)(0.10) + ($400,000/$850,000)(0.085).

The financial adviser's estimate of an 8 percent portfolio expected rate of return was wrong for two reasons. First, he used the assets' market values instead of their after-tax values to measure each asset's weight in the portfolio. Second, he did not adjust the pre-tax expected returns on stocks held in taxable accounts for taxes. For this active stock investor, the after-tax expected return is 8.5 percent or [10%(1 − 0.15)].

VALUATION OF OTHER ASSETS

This chapter explained how we can estimate the after-tax value of most financial assets. This section discusses the valuation of other assets such as U.S. savings bonds that are subject to a separate section of the tax code. It also provides another example of the tax adjustment for embedded capital gains.

Consider the valuation of a U.S. savings bond. Suppose someone invested $1,000 in a savings bond 20 years earlier when interest rates were much higher. Its market value (that is, redemption value) is $4,240. If retained, it will earn a 7.5 percent annual tax-deferred return for up to ten more years. Due to today's much lower interest rates, this individual plans to retain these funds in the savings bond for the full ten years. Today's after-tax value is $3,430, $4,240 less the $810 tax liability on the $3,240 of tax-deferred return. As explained in Appendix C, even though the tax liability will not be paid for ten years, the after-tax value is the same as if the deferred returns were realized today and taxes were paid at 25 percent.

An individual owns undeveloped land. It was bought years earlier at $250,000 and its market value (perhaps adjusted for real estate commissions at the sale) is estimated at $400,000. It is estimated that the land will be sold in 15 years and the long-term capital gain tax rate will be 20 percent at that time. The market value contains an expected future tax liability of $30,000 or [(0.20) $150,000]. So, the after-tax value is $370,000.

Notice, in this example, to calculate *today's* after-tax value we need to reduce the *current* market value for the *current* embedded tax liability. The sales price 15 years hence might be considerably more than $400,000. But it does not make sense to reduce *today's* market value for the tax liability on *anticipated* future capital gains.

To estimate the after-tax value of tax-deferred accounts, we needed to estimate the ordinary income tax rate in retirement. To estimate the after-tax value of stock with an embedded unrealized capital gain, we needed to estimate the eventual tax liability, if any, on the embedded capital gain. The key is to remember that it is better to adjust the asset's market value for a reasonable estimate of the tax liability than to ignore taxes entirely. It is better to calculate an after-tax asset allocation based on estimates of assets' after-tax values than to use the traditional approach that implicitly assumes taxes do not exist.

The next chapter examines the choice of saving vehicles when someone is saving for retirement. Chapter 2 showed that tax-deferred accounts and Roths are more tax-favored than taxable accounts or non-qualified annuities. Chapter 4 helps individuals who have the choice decide whether to save for retirement in a tax-deferred account or a tax-exempt Roth. The introduction of the Roth 401(k) and Roth 403(b) means that more individuals will face this decision. In addition, the impact of matching contributions is also examined.

SUMMARY

Conceptually, it is easy to understand why we should use after-tax values when calculating individuals' after-tax asset allocations. The traditional approach of calculating asset allocations ignores taxes and, thus, implicitly assumes taxes do not exist. In contrast, the after-tax approach adjusts assets' market values for embedded tax liabilities. Therefore, it compares after-tax dollars to after-tax dollars. Although easy to understand conceptually, there can be problems when trying to apply this concept. In particular, we usually need to estimate the ordinary income tax rate in retirement and may need to make other estimates. However, it is better to make reasonable estimates of these tax adjustments than to pretend that taxes do not exist.

To calculate an after-tax asset allocation, we must first convert all assets' market values to after-tax values. That is, we must adjust the market values for embedded tax liabilities. For assets held in tax-exempt Roths, there is no adjustment for taxes. For assets held in tax-deferred accounts, we should multiply their pre-tax market values by $(1 - t_n)$ to convert the funds to after-tax values, where t_n is the expected tax rate in retirement. For assets held in taxable accounts, when the market value equals the cost basis, the after-tax value is the same as the market value. When the market value exceeds the cost basis, we should decrease the market value for the expected tax liability associated with the embedded capital gain. Remember, if the asset is not expected to be sold until receiving the step-up in basis at death, then the tax liability will be zero. Similarly, when the market value is less than the cost basis, we should increase the market value for the tax savings on the embedded loss. For assets held in non-qualified annuities, the process of adjusting market value for taxes is similar to the process for assets held in taxable accounts with two exceptions. First, the applicable tax rate is the ordinary income tax rate instead of the long-term capital gain rate. Second, there should be no adjustment for embedded capital losses, since realized losses in non-qualified annuities can seldom be used to reduce taxable income.

In this chapter, we have established the following principles and investment implications:

- For an asset held in a tax-exempt Roth, its market value is its after-tax value.
- For an asset held in a tax-deferred account, its after-tax value is its market value multiplied by $(1 - t_n)$, where t_n is the expected tax rate in retirement.
- For an asset held in a taxable account, its after-tax value is its market value less the expected tax liability associated with any unrealized gain or plus the tax savings associated with any unrealized loss.
- For an asset held in a non-qualified annuity, its after-tax value is its market value less the tax liability associated with any tax-deferred returns.
- It is more complex to calculate an individual's after-tax asset allocation, because it usually requires an estimate of the ordinary income tax rate in retirement. In addition, it may require other estimates. However, it is better to face the reality that taxes exist and to make reasonable adjustments for them than to pretend that taxes do not exist.

ENDNOTE

[1] Annuity losses can be deducted against ordinary income as miscellaneous itemized deductions. Therefore, to use them the individual must 1) itemize deductions and 2) miscellaneous itemized deductions must exceed 2 percent of Adjusted Gross Income. In practice, these criteria are seldom met.

4 Choice of Savings Vehicles When Saving for Retirement

This chapter is designed to help individuals select the best savings vehicles when saving for retirement. Chapter 2 concluded that tax-exempt Roths and tax-deferred accounts are much more tax-favored than taxable accounts or non-qualified annuities. So, in general, when saving for retirement, we should save all we can in these most favored saving vehicles. However, there are times when we must decide whether to save in a tax-exempt Roth or a tax-deferred account. This chapter examines that decision.

A key factor in this decision will be a comparison between the marginal tax rate in the contribution year, t, and the marginal tax rate in the withdrawal year, t_n. It could be a decision to 1) save in a Roth IRA or a traditional IRA, 2) save in a Roth 401(k) or a 401(k), 3) save in a Roth 403(b) or a 403(b), or 4) convert funds from a traditional IRA to a Roth IRA. In each case, a comparison of t and t_n is usually the first criterion when making the decision. This chapter also examines how the presence of a matching contribution should affect the choice of savings vehicles. Then, it discusses other factors besides the comparison of t and t_n that might influence the decision to save in a tax-exempt Roth or a tax-deferred account.

TWO TYPES OF QUESTIONS

This book examines two separate questions. The first is, "How should we calculate an individual's asset allocation?" Chapters 1 and 3 explained the logic of calculating an individual's after-tax asset allocation and how it should be calculated. To calculate an after-tax asset allocation, pre-tax funds in tax-deferred accounts should be converted to after-tax funds by multiplying by $(1 - t_n)$. The applicable tax rate is t_n, the expected tax rate in retirement, while the current tax rate, t, is irrelevant.

The second question—and the question addressed in this chapter—is whether someone should save first in a Roth and then a tax-deferred account or vice versa. When answering this question, the first factor in the analysis and usually the deciding factor is a comparison of relative sizes of t and t_n. For this question, both t and t_n are relevant.

TAX-EXEMPT AND TAX-DEFERRED ACCOUNTS

Most of the analysis in the chapter concerns the choice between saving in a tax-deferred account or a tax-exempt account. Several countries have tax-deferred accounts, but relatively few have tax-exempt accounts. The United States has both tax-deferred accounts and Roths. Canada already has tax-deferred accounts and will have tax-exempt accounts beginning in 2009. So, the analysis in this chapter should be of special interest to financial advisers in the U.S. and Canada.

Tax-deferred and tax-exempt accounts in the U.S. In the U.S., tax-deferred accounts include 401(k)s, 403(b)s, traditional (deductible) IRAs, Keoghs, and SEP-IRAs and tax-exempt accounts include Roth IRAs, Roth 401(k)s, and Roth 403(b)s. Beginning in 2006, for-profit firms are allowed (but not required) to have a Roth 401(k) in addition to the traditional 401(k) plan. Not-for-profit firms are allowed (but not required) to have a Roth 403(b) in addition to the traditional 403(b) plan. In 2008, employees of firms with a Roth 401(k) and 401(k) can contribute up to $15,500 (or $20,500 if age 50 or over) in the Roth 401(k) or 401(k) or a combination of each. A parallel statement applies to employees of firms with a Roth 403(b) and 403(b).[1]

Contributions to 401(k) and 403(b) plans are tax deductible in the contribution year, returns grow tax deferred, and withdrawals are fully taxable at ordinary income tax rates. In contrast, contributions to Roth 401(k) and Roth 403(b) plans are not deductible in the contribution year, but returns are tax exempt (as long as the account has been in existences for at least five years, and the owner is at least age 59.5).

Although the Roth IRA has been around since 1998, I suspect the introduction of the Roth 401(k) and Roth 403(b) will dramatically increase the amount of funds in tax-exempt Roths. This is because many high income individuals earn too much income to qualify for contributions to a Roth IRA, but these income limits do not restrict contributions to a Roth 401(k) or a Roth 403(b). Moreover, in 2008 the maximum contribution to a Roth IRA is only $4,000 (or $5,000 if over 50), while the maximum contributions to a Roth 401(k) or a Roth 403(b) are about four times as large at $15,500 (or $20,500 if over 50).

Tax-deferred and tax-exempt accounts in Canada. In Canada, tax-deferred plans are called Registered Retirement Savings Plans (RRSPs). Beginning in 2009, they will have tax-exempt accounts called Tax-Free Savings Accounts (TFSAs). In 2008, the maximum contribution limit to the tax-deductible RRSP is $20,000. However, that maximum is increased for any unused portions of the prior year's contribution limit. So, individuals who did not make any contribution toward the $19,000 limit in 2007 could contribute $39,000 in 2008. Like tax-deferred accounts in other countries, contributions to an RRSP are tax deductible in the contribution year, returns grow tax-deferred, and withdrawals are taxable as ordinary income.

Beginning in 2009, each Canadian age 18 or older may save up to $5,000 per year in tax-exempt Tax Free Savings Accounts (TFSAs). Furthermore, one partner could also contribute $5,000 for his or her spouse or common-law partner. TFSAs have important advantages compared to investments in tax-exempt Roths in the U.S. First, unused portions of annual contributions accumulate through the years. So, someone who does not make a TFSA contribution in 2009 or 2010 could make a $15,000 contribution in 2011. Second, there are no restrictions on withdrawals. Withdrawals at any age are tax exempt and individuals can make contributions later to offset such withdrawals. For example, a 25-year-old could withdraw $22,000 in 2014 to buy a car and reinvest that amount in, say, 2016. Furthermore, that $22,000 contribution in 2016 would not affect the usual $5,000 contribution limit for that year. Consequently, unlike tax-exempt accounts in the U.S., TFSAs are not designed only for or primarily for people saving for retirement. For additional information, search the Internet for "tax free savings accounts" or see www. cra-arc.gc.ca/agency/budget/2008/taxfree-e.html.

Although there are differences between tax-deferred and tax-exempt accounts in the U.S. and Canada, they each allow tax free accumulation of returns for someone saving for retirement. The remainder of this chapter is concerned with an individual's choice to save for retirement within a tax-deferred or tax-exempt account. The examples assume the investor is in the U.S., but the analysis would be similar for someone in Canada. The obvious difference is that the TFSA should appeal not only to individuals saving for retirement, but also to individuals saving for a goal before attaining retirement age.

COMPARING TAX-DEFERRED AND TAX-EXEMPT ACCOUNTS

Table 2.3 (p. 22) presented the effective tax rates on funds invested in bonds or stocks across four savings vehicles: tax-exempt Roths, tax-deferred accounts, taxable accounts, and non-qualified annuities. The most tax-favored savings vehicles by far are the Roths and tax-deferred accounts. In general, when saving for retirement, we should save all we can in these most tax-favored savings vehicles.

For example, I save all I can in these savings vehicles through my university job. In addition, I save all I can from my side business, which includes income from consulting and writing. Also, when eligible, my wife and I save additional funds in a Roth IRA. However, for my university job, I must decide whether to save in a 403(b) or a Roth 403(b). This chapter concentrates on the decision.

This section presents two examples that indicate the importance of the comparison between the tax rate in the contribution year, t, and the tax rate in the withdrawal year, t_n. Table 4.1 summarizes the first example. Peggy is willing to reduce this year's spending by $690 and will save the funds until retirement. She is trying to decide whether to save in a Roth or a tax-deferred account. Table 4.1 assumes she has a 31 percent marginal tax rate this year and will have a 31 percent tax rate when she withdraws the funds in retirement. If she saves $690 of *after-tax* funds in a Roth, it would reduce the amount she could spend this year by $690. If she saves $1,000 of *pre-tax* funds in a tax-deferred account, it would reduce her taxable income by $1,000, which would reduce her taxes by $310. So, the $1,000 contribution to the tax-deferred account would also reduce the amount of money she could spend this year by $690. Table 4.1 separates this $1,000 of pre-tax funds into two parts: $310 of tax savings and Peggy's $690 of after-tax funds.

Whether she saves in the Roth or tax-deferred account, she will invest in the same asset and withdraw the funds in retirement. The investment could be a stock fund, bond fund, or any other investment. Without loss of generality, assume the investment doubles between now and retirement. At retirement, the $690 in the Roth would be worth $1,380. She could withdraw the $1,380 of after-tax funds and buy $1,380 of goods and services. If she invested in the tax-deferred account, at retirement the account would be worth $2,000 before taxes. At withdrawal, she would pay $620 or [$2,000 (0.31)] in taxes, and she could use the $1,380 of after-tax funds to buy the same amount of goods and services. In this example, whether she saves in a Roth or tax-deferred account, she will reduce this year's spending by $690 and finance $1,380 of goods and services in retirement.

Table 4.1. Savings in Tax-Exempt and Tax-Deferred Accounts: 31% Tax Rates before and in Retirement

Savings Vehicle	Original Investment	Retirement Wealth
Tax-Exempt Roth	$690 after-tax funds	$1,380 after-tax funds
Tax-Deferred Account	$1,000 pre-tax funds – $310 tax savings $690 after-tax funds	$2,000 pre-tax funds – $620 taxes $1,380 after-tax funds

Peggy has a 31 percent tax rate in both the contribution year and withdrawal year in retirement.

Table 4.2 summarizes a second possibility. In this example, she has a 31 percent tax rate this year but will have a 25 percent tax rate in retirement. As before, she is willing to reduce this year's spending by $690. If she saves in the Roth, she invests $690 today and it would be worth $1,380 after taxes in retirement. If she saves in the tax-deferred account, she invests $1,000 of pre-tax funds today and it would be worth $2,000 before taxes or $1,500 after taxes in retirement after paying taxes of $500, [$2,000(0.25)].

There are important investment lessons that come from these tables. First, from Table 4.1, when the tax rate in the contribution year, t, is the same as the tax rate in the withdrawal year, t_n, the contribution in the tax-deferred account grows effectively tax free.

Traditionally, people have thought about tax-deferred accounts as growing tax deferred. However, when $t = t_n$, the tax savings grows to pay the full tax bill at withdrawal. In Table 4.1, the $310 tax savings grew to pay the full tax bill of $620 at withdrawal. In general, the first factor to consider when deciding whether to save in a Roth or tax-deferred account is the relative sizes of t and t_n. Since $t = t_n$ in Table 4.1, this factor suggests that Peggy should be indifferent to saving $690 in the Roth or $1,000 in the tax-deferred account. Later in this chapter, we will consider other factors that may influence her decision to save in a Roth or tax-deferred account.

Second, when the tax rate in the withdrawal year is less than the tax rate in the contribution year, $t_n < t$, the effective tax rate on the tax-deferred account is negative.[2] From Table 4.2, the $310 tax savings in the contribution year grows to $620 at retirement, but only $500 is needed to pay the full tax bill. So, the investor keeps the remaining $120. Since $t_n < t$, this factor suggests that Peggy should save $1,000 in the tax-deferred account instead of saving $690 in the Roth.

Table 4.2. Savings in Tax-Exempt and Tax-Deferred Accounts: 31% Tax Rate before and 25% in Retirement		
Savings Vehicle	**Original Investment**	**Retirement Wealth**
Tax-Exempt Roth	$690 after-tax funds	$1,380 after-tax funds
Tax-Deferred Account	$1,000 pre-tax funds −$310 tax savings $690 after-tax funds	$2,000 pre-tax funds −$500 taxes $1,500 after-tax funds

Peggy has a 31 percent tax rate in the contribution year but 25 percent rate in withdrawal year in retirement.

CHOICE OF SAVINGS VEHICLES

This section extends the analysis in the prior section by considering two examples where the individual investor will receive a matching contribution from the firm.

Example 1. For the first example, suppose Peggy must choose between saving in her firm's 401(k) or Roth 401(k) plan. She is willing to reduce spending this year by $6,900 and will save those funds for retirement. Moreover, the firm matches her annual contribution dollar for dollar up to $4,000. Table 4.3 examines her optimal saving strategy, assuming she has a 31 percent marginal tax rate this year and will have a 25 percent, 31 percent, or 35 percent tax rate in retirement. It shows the after-tax values in retirement *from her contributions* (but not the matching contributions) assuming the cumulative pre-tax return before retirement is 100 percent.

Table 4.3. Comparing After-tax Wealth in Retirement from Saving in Tax-Exempt Roth versus Tax-Deferred Account

Savings Vehicle	Retirement Tax Rates		
	25%	**31%**	**35%**
401(k)	$20,000 before taxes −$5,000 taxes $15,000 after taxes	$20,000 before taxes −$6,200 taxes $13,800 after taxes	$20,000 before taxes −$7,000 taxes $13,000 after taxes
Roth 401(k)	$13,800 after taxes	$13,800 after taxes	$13,800 after taxes

She could contribute either $6,900 of after-tax funds to the tax-exempt Roth 401(k) or $10,000 of pre-tax funds to the 401(k). Both investments will decrease this year's spending by $6,900. Furthermore, both investments will result in a $4,000 matching contribution from the firm. Whether Peggy saves in a Roth 401(k) or 401(k), the firm's $4,000 matching contribution will go into a 401(k) in her name. Thus the $4,000 matching contribution consists of pre-tax funds and, in retirement, she will owe taxes on the full amount of withdrawals from this account. Table 4.3 ignores the ending after-tax wealth from this matching contribution, since it is the same whether she saves in a Roth 401(k) or 401(k).

From Table 4.3, if she expects withdrawals in retirement to be subject to a 25 percent marginal tax rate, then she should contribute $10,000 of pre-tax funds this year to the 401(k). If the asset's cumulative return is 100 percent by retirement, these funds would be worth $20,000 before taxes, but $15,000 after taxes. In contrast, if she saved $6,900 this year in a Roth 401(k), it would only be worth $13,800 after taxes in retirement. When $t_n < t$, the tax-deferred account produces the higher after-tax wealth.

If she expects withdrawals in retirement to be subject to a 31 percent marginal tax rate, then she should be indifferent between saving $6,900 in the Roth 401(k) or $10,000 in the 401(k). Both savings amounts would be worth $13,800 after taxes in retirement. The next section will discuss factors besides the relative sizes of t and t_n that may influence her decision to save in the 401(k) or Roth 401(k).

If she expects withdrawals in retirement to be subject to a 35 percent marginal tax rate, then she should contribute $6,900 of after-tax funds this year to the Roth 401(k). These funds would be worth $13,800 after taxes in retirement. In contrast, if she saved this year in the 401(k), the funds would be worth $20,000 before taxes but only $13,000 after taxes.

Example 2. Let us consider a second example. Suppose George is a recent college graduate who expects to be in higher tax brackets in future years, including in retirement. He is in the 15 percent tax bracket this year and is willing to reduce consumption this year by $4,000. His firm has a 401(k) plan with a matching contribution of up to $4,000, but it does not have a Roth 401(k) plan. However, he is eligible to contribute up to $4,000 to a Roth IRA. What is his optimal choice of savings vehicles?

His first choice of savings vehicles should be to save $4,000 of pre-tax funds in the 401(k) to receive the matching contributions. Including the match, he begins with $8,000 in contributions—his and the firm's. He begins with twice as many pre-tax dollars and, at withdrawal, has twice as many after-tax dollars compared to the 401(k) without the matching contribution. Even if the firm only matches contributions at the rate of 50 cents on the dollar, matching contributions are usually too good a deal to pass up.[3]

Since George's $4,000 contribution to the 401(k) will reduce this year's taxes by $600, it will only reduce the amount he can spend this year by $3,400. To repeat, he is willing to reduce spending this . year by $4,000. So, he must decide between saving 1) an additional $600 of after-tax funds in the Roth IRA or 2) an additional $600 of after-tax funds [or $706 = $600/(1 – 0.15) of pre-tax funds] in the 401(k). Since he expects to be in a higher tax bracket in retirement, he should save in the Roth IRA. This second example illustrates that the choice of savings vehicles may not be limited to the firm's 401(k) or Roth 401(k). Rather, in this example, the optimal combination of savings vehicles used the firm's 401(k) up to the matching contribution amount and the Roth IRA for additional contributions.

OTHER FACTORS THAT MAY INFLUENCE THE CHOICE OF SAVINGS VEHICLES

Although the comparison between the tax rate in the contribution year, t, and the tax rate in the withdrawal year, t_n, is usually a key factor in the choice of saving vehicles, there are other factors that may influence this decision. This section discusses five of these factors.

1. The maximum annual contribution limit is the same for a 401(k) and Roth 401(k), but this limit does not take into consideration taxes. For 2008, someone under 50 could contribute up to $15,500 to a 401(k) or a Roth 401(k). But a $15,500 contribution of *after-tax* funds to a Roth 401(k) is effectively a larger contribution than a $15,500 contribution of *pre-tax* funds to a 401(k). In the example in Table 4.1, Peggy was in the 31 percent tax bracket in the contribution and withdrawal years, and a $690 contribution to a Roth produced the same after-tax wealth as a $1,000 contribution to a tax-deferred account. In that example, the maximum contribution limit was not a factor. But when it is a

factor, the same $15,500 contribution limit is effectively a larger contribution if it can be made with after-tax funds instead of pre-tax funds. This factor favors an investment in a Roth 401(k) instead of a 401(k) and a Roth IRA instead of a traditional IRA.

2. There are no required minimum distributions in a Roth IRA, while there are RMDs in a tax-deferred account. There are RMDs in a Roth 401(k) and a Roth 403(b). To avoid this problem, at retirement you can roll the Roth 401(k) or Roth 403(b) into a Roth IRA. So, effectively, there need be no RMDs from any of the tax-exempt Roths. This factor favors an investment in a Roth. In Table 4.1, Peggy may prefer to save in a Roth instead of a tax-deferred account because of this factor.

3. As discussed in Appendix B, distributions from the tax-deferred accounts may cause someone's Social Security benefits to be taxable or taxable at a higher rate. This factor favors Roths.

4. Everything else the same, someone who has most of his retirement funds in tax-deferred accounts might prefer to save in a Roth today. Because most of his funds will be taxed at retirement tax rates, he may prefer to save in a Roth today, for diversification purposes, since taxes on these funds would be paid at today's rate. This is a tax diversification play. Diversify your funds so some will be paid at today's rates and some at the uncertain tax rates in retirement. Since most individuals have substantially more assets in tax-deferred accounts than in Roths, this factor usually favors the Roths.

5. If someone itemizes deductions for income tax purposes, his deductions for business expenses, casualty losses, investment expenses, and medical expenses may be affected by the choice between saving in a Roth or tax-deferred account. For example, medical expenses exceeding 7.5 percent of Adjusted Gross Income (AGI) are deductible. If he saves in a tax-deferred account, he will have a lower AGI and, therefore, more of these expenses will be deductible this year. Although saving in a tax-deferred account will lower his AGI this year, it will raise his AGI after he reaches age 70.5 due to required minimum distributions.

Although there is a trade-off, individuals whose current income levels affect their ability to deduct business expenses, casualty losses, investment expenses, and medical expenses may prefer to save in a tax-deferred account.

For a more complete discussion of the decision to save in a tax-deferred account or Roth, see Waltenberger, Rothermich, and Reichenstein, "The Expanding 'Roth' Retirement Account," TIAA-CREF Institute, March 2006, at www.tiaa-crefinstitute.org/research/trends/tr030106.html.

The next chapter compares a tax-oblivious traditional mean variance optimization to a tax-aware after-tax optimization for a hypothetical individual investor. The traditional mean variance optimization 1) fails to distinguish between pre-tax funds and after-tax funds and 2) does not adjust for the fact that, when held in a taxable account, the government bears some of an asset's pre-tax risk. The latter concept was discussed in Chapter 2. In contrast, the after-tax optimization 1) is based on after-tax balances so it distinguishes between pre-tax and after-tax funds and 2) it adjusts each asset's risk to reflect the risk borne by the individual investor. As we shall see, these adjustments have important effects on the optimal asset allocation. Moreover, this framework clearly illustrates why someone should locate bonds in retirement accounts and stocks in taxable accounts, while attaining his or her target asset allocation.

SUMMARY

The goal of this chapter was to help an individual decide whether to save in tax-exempt Roths or tax-deferred accounts. A similar question is whether an individual should convert funds from a traditional IRA to a Roth IRA. A key factor in these decisions is the relative sizes of the current year's marginal tax rate, t, and the expected marginal tax rate when the funds are withdrawn during retirement, t_n. In general, when the retirement tax rate is less than the current tax rate (that is, $t_n < t$) then the individual should save in a tax-deferred account before a Roth. In general, when the retirement tax rate exceeds the current tax rate (that is, $t_n > t$) then the individual should save in a Roth before a tax-deferred account. When the two rates are the same or even close, other factors may play a deciding role.

Most of these other factors favor saving in Roths before tax-deferred accounts. They include 1) the maximum annual contribution is effectively larger when it is made with after-tax dollars instead of pre-tax dollars; 2) the lack of required minimum distributions on Roth IRAs (and by rolling Roth 401(k)s and Roth 403(b)s into Roth IRAs, required minimum distributions on the Roth 401(k)s and Roth 403(b)s can also be avoided); and 3) distributions from tax-deferred accounts may increase taxes on Social Security benefits. On the other hand, individuals whose current taxable income levels are so high that it affects their ability to deduct business expenses, casualty losses, investment expenses, and medical expenses may prefer to save in a tax-deferred account before a Roth.

In this chapter, we established or restated the following principles and investment implications:

- When saving for retirement, savings held in tax-exempt Roths like the Roth IRA and tax-deferred accounts like the 401(k) are much more tax-favored than savings held in taxable accounts or non-qualified annuities. Therefore, when saving for retirement, individuals should generally save all they are allowed to save or all they can afford to save in these most tax-favored savings vehicles.
- Frequently, individuals must decide whether to save in a tax-deferred account or a tax-exempt Roth. When there is a matching contribution, the individual should make sure he gets all matching contributions. For example, suppose George works for a firm that offers a 401(k) but not a Roth 401(k), and it will match George's contributions to the 401(k) up to $4,000. If he is eligible for a Roth IRA, he must decide whether to save in a 401(k) or a

Roth IRA. His first savings should go to the 401(k) until he gets all matching contributions. Additional savings beyond the match may go to the 401(k) or Roth IRA.

- Consider an individual who must decide whether to save in a tax-deferred account or a Roth and the decision does not affect a matching contribution. This would include George's decision to save additional amounts (beyond the $4,000 necessary to attain all matching contributions) in a Roth IRA or 401(k). The first criterion is usually to compare the marginal tax rates in the contribution year, t, and the withdrawal year, t_n. When $t_n < t$, the individual usually should save in the tax-deferred account, and vice versa.

- When t and t_n are equal or close, other factors usually come into play. Most of these other factors favor investments in Roths. They include 1) the maximum annual contribution is effectively larger when it is made with after-tax dollars; 2) the lack of required minimum distributions on Roth IRAs and effectively on Roth 401(k)s and Roth 403(b)s; and 3) distributions from tax-deferred accounts may increase taxes on Social Security benefits.

ENDNOTES

[1] In the United States, for 2008, the annual contribution limits are the smaller of earned income (for example, wages and salaries) or $15,500 for 401(k), Roth 401(k), 403(b), Roth 403(b), and 457. In addition, there is a $5,000 annual catch-up contribution limit for those at least age 50. For the SIMPLE plan, the annual contribution limit is the smaller of earned income or $10,500 with a catch-up contribution limit of $2,500. For the Roth IRA, the annual contribution limit is the smaller of earned income or $5,000 for singles with a catch-up contribution of $1,000. For a married couple filing jointly, each partner may contribute the smaller of earned income or $5,000 with a catch-up contribution of $1,000. Furthermore, a non-income-earning partner can, in essence, use $5,000 of earned income of the working partner. For the Roth IRA, there are income limits that may affect the maximum contribution. Roth IRA contributions are phased out for singles with modified adjusted gross income (MAGI) between $101,000

and $116,000; below $101,000, singles may make the maximum contribution, but the contribution limit is phased out as MAGI rises from $101,000 to $116,000, and no contributions are allowed for MAGI above $116,000. For married couples filing jointly, Roth IRA contributions are phased out for MAGI between $159,000 and $169,000. After 2008, all contribution limits and phase out ranges for every type of account—for example, 401(k), Roth 401(k), SIMPLE, and Roth IRA—will be adjusted for inflation.

[2] For clarification, in Chapter 2 we concluded that the effective tax rate on tax-deferred accounts was zero. The negative tax rate here is not a contradiction. Since this year's tax rate, t, is 31 percent, the $1,000 contribution reduced this year's spending by $690. In Table 4.2, the $690 more than doubled to $1,500. So, when we compare reduced spending this year to increased spending in retirement, the applicable tax rate is t and the effective tax rate was negative. However, when calculating the asset allocation, the $1,000 contribution of pre-tax funds this year is worth $750 after taxes. Since the funds will be withdrawn in retirement, the applicable tax rate is t_n and the $1,000 of pre-tax funds is worth $750 or $1,000(1 - t_n)$ after taxes, while the government effectively owns t_n of the current principal. The after-tax funds grow from $1,000(1 - t_n)$ today to $1,000(1 - t_n)(1 + r)^n$ at retirement, so it effectively grows tax exempt.

[3] As discussed in this chapter, the proper comparison is between George making a $3,400 contribution of after-tax funds to a tax-exempt account or a $4,000 contribution of his pre-tax funds to a tax-deferred account, because both contributions reduce the amount he can spend this year by $3,400. In retirement, the after-tax value of the tax-exempt account will be $3,400(1+r)^n$, while the after-tax value of George's $4,000 contribution plus the $2,000 matching contribution will be $6,000(1+r)^n(1 - t_n)$, where r is the pre-tax rate of return and n is the length of the investment horizon. As long as t_n, the retirement tax rate, is less than 43.3 percent, George should seek the company matching contribution before investing in the Roth IRA.

5 | *Mean Variance Optimization and Asset Location with Taxes*

This chapter demonstrates differences between a tax-oblivious traditional mean variance optimization and a tax-aware after-tax optimization. We shall see that once portfolios have been adjusted for taxes, there is usually a strong asset location preference. Asset location refers to the decision to locate bonds in tax-exempt Roths and tax-deferred accounts and stocks in taxable accounts or vice versa, while maintaining the target asset allocation.

REVIEW

Let's review what we learned in Chapter 2. It examined how the choice of savings vehicles affects the portion of returns received by and risk borne by individual investors. Table 2.1 is partially reproduced as Table 5.1.

In a tax-exempt Roth, the individual investor receives all returns and bears all risk. In a tax-deferred account, the individual effectively owns $(1 - t_n)$ of principal, but receives all returns and bears all risk. Each $1 of pre-tax funds in a tax-deferred account is like $(1 - t_n)$ dollar of after-tax funds in a Roth. But that after-tax dollar grows, effectively tax exempt, from $(1 - t_n)$ today to the compounding formula $(1 - t_n)(1 + r)^n$ in n years, where r is the pre-tax rate of return and n is the length of the investment horizon.

Table 5.1. Principal Owned, Returns Received, and Risk Borne by Individual Investors in Tax-exempt Roths, Tax-deferred Accounts, Taxable Accounts, and Non-qualified Annuities

	Principal	Returns	Risk
Tax-exempt Roths			
bonds and stocks	100%	100%	100%
Tax-deferred Accounts			
bonds and stocks	$(1 - t_n)$	100%	100%
Taxable Accounts			
bonds	100%	$(1 - t)$	$(1 - t)$
stocks, active investor	100%	$(1 - t_c)$	$(1 - t_c)$
Non-qualified Annuities			
bonds and stocks	100%	$\geq(1 - t_n)$	$\geq(1 - t_n)$

The ordinary income tax rate is t in years before withdrawal and t_n in the withdrawal year, and the tax rate on long-term capital gains and qualified dividends is t_c in all years. Tax-exempt Roths include a Roth IRA, while tax-deferred accounts include 401(k)s, 403(b)s, Keoghs, and SEP-IRAs. Source: Adapted from Reichenstein (2007b)

In a taxable account, the portion of returns received by and risk borne by the individual investor varies with the underlying asset. For bonds, the individual investor receives $(1 - t)$ of returns and bears approximately $(1 - t)$ of risk, where t is the ordinary income tax rate. For stocks, the portion varies with the stock management style. For now, let's assume the individual is an active investor who realizes capital gains as soon as they are eligible for the long-term gains tax treatment. This individual receives $(1 - t_c)$ of returns and bears $(1 - t_c)$ of risk, where t_c is the long-term capital gain tax rate.

In a non-qualified annuity, the portion of returns received by and risk borne by the individual varies with the investment horizon. For a multi-year horizon, the individual receives and bears more than $(1 - t_n)$ of the asset's returns and risk.

For this chapter, the key insight is the portion of an asset's risk received by and return borne by individual investors varies with the savings vehicle. For bonds and stocks held in Roths and tax-deferred accounts, that portion is 100 percent. For funds held in taxable accounts, that portion is $(1 - t)$ for bonds and $(1 - t_c)$ for stocks held by an active investor. For bonds and stocks held for multi-year horizons in non-qualified annuities, that portion is more than $(1 - t_n)$.

In the next section, we contrast a tax-oblivious traditional mean variance optimization to a tax-aware after-tax optimization for a hypothetical investor. The contrast provides important insights into the asset location decision.

MEAN VARIANCE OPTIMIZATIONS

Each individual must make an asset allocation decision and an asset location decision. Asset allocation in the examples presented here refers to the allocation of funds between stocks and bonds. The asset location decision refers to the decision to locate bonds in Roths and tax-deferred accounts and stocks in taxable accounts or vice versa, while maintaining the target asset allocation. (We defer discussion of non-qualified annuities until later in the chapter.)

Many financial planners use the ideas of modern portfolio theory as first espoused by Harry Markowitz (1952). Some planners produce objective estimates of expected returns and standard deviations for each asset class, estimate correlation coefficients for each pair of asset classes, and insert them into an optimizer to estimate an optimal portfolio. Other planners apply the key ideas, but subjectively estimate an optimal portfolio. This section uses an optimizer because it objectively shows that, except for extreme cases, individual investors should locate bonds in Roths and tax-deferred accounts and stocks in taxable accounts, while maintaining their target asset allocation.

In this section, we initially assume the individual is an active stock investor. He has $480,000 of pre-tax funds in tax-deferred accounts, $20,000 of after-tax funds in Roths, and $500,000 in taxable accounts. For assets held in taxable accounts, the market values equal the cost bases. We first perform a traditional mean variance optimization and then an after-tax optimization.

Table 5.2 presents the traditional mean variance optimization. Since the traditional approach ignores taxes, the optimization only considers the pre-tax returns and pre-tax risks. Bonds' pre-tax returns and standard deviation are 6 percent and 8 percent, while stocks' are 8 percent and 16 percent. Moreover, the traditional approach assumes taxes do not exist, so it fails to consider the embedded tax

Table 5.2. Traditional Mean Variance Optimization for Active Investor

	Market Values	Optimal Weights	Pre-tax Expected Returns	Pre-tax Standard Deviation
Stocks	$500,000	50%	8%	16%
Bonds	+$500,000 $1,000,000	50%	6%	8%

Maximize Utility = $ER - SD^2/RT$, where ER is portfolio expected returns, SD is portfolio standard deviation, and RT, the investor's risk tolerance, is set at 0.96, because this is the RT that makes the optimal asset mix 50 percent bonds and 50 percent stocks. The utility function says the investor likes returns—i.e., utility increases with ER—but dislikes risk—utility decreases with an increase in SD. The SD^2/RT is a reduction from ER for risk. Thus, if ER is 0.07 and SD^2/RT is 0.025, the investor would be indifferent between a risk-free return of 0.045 and an ER of 0.07 and SD^2/RT of 0.025. Constraints: $S, B \geq 0$; $S + B = 1$, where S and B denote the weights in stocks and bonds. The correlation coefficient between stock and bond returns is 0.2. Optimization was performed in Excel.

liability in tax-deferred accounts. It only considers the market values of the assets and views the portfolio as worth $1 million. We set the correlation coefficient between bond and stock returns at 0.2 and the risk tolerance at 0.96 because this is the level that sets the asset allocation at 50 percent bonds and 50 percent stocks.

Because the traditional approach ignores taxes, it is silent on the issue of asset location. Therefore, it would consider the following portfolios to be equivalent: 1) $500,000 in stocks in Roths and tax-deferred accounts and $500,000 in bonds in taxable accounts and 2) $500,000 in bonds in Roths and tax-deferred accounts and $500,000 in stocks in taxable accounts. In summary, for this risk tolerance level, the traditional approach's optimal asset allocation is 50 percent bonds and 50 percent stocks, while this approach is silent about the optimal asset location.

Table 5.3 presents the after-tax mean variance optimization. The first step in performing an after-tax optimization is to calculate the size of his after-tax portfolio. The top half of this table presents this calculation. It assumes he is an active investor in the 35 percent ordinary income tax bracket and 15 percent capital gain bracket. His after-tax portfolio contains $312,000 of after-tax funds in tax-deferred accounts, $20,000 in Roths, and $500,000 in taxable accounts for an $832,000 after-tax portfolio.

The lower half of this table presents the after-tax mean variance optimization. It assumes the same pre-tax returns and risks and same risk tolerance as for the traditional optimization. These pre-tax returns and risk are also the after-tax returns and risk for bonds and stock when held in Roths and tax-deferred accounts. When held in taxable accounts, bonds' after-tax return is 3.9 percent or $[6\%(1 - 0.35)]$ and the after-tax risk is 5.2 percent or $[8\%(1 - 0.35)]$. For this active investor, stocks' after-tax return is 6.8 percent or $[8\%(1 - 0.15)]$ and the after-tax risk is 13.6 percent. Even though this after-tax optimization only considers two assets—bonds and stocks—there are effectively four assets

Table 5.3. After-tax Mean Variance Optimization for Active Investor				
	Market Values	**After-tax Values**	**Savings Vehicle**	
	$480,000	$312,000	tax-deferred accounts	
	$20,000	$20,000	tax-exempt Roths	
	+ $500,000	+ $500,000	taxable accounts	
	$1,000,000	$832,000		
	After-tax Values	**Optimal Weights**	**After-tax Expected Returns**	**After-tax Standard Deviation**
Stocks in TDAs and Roths	$0	0%	8.0%	16%
Bonds in TDAs and Roths	$332,000	39.9%	6.0%	8%
Stocks in taxable accounts	$500,000	60.1%	6.8%	13.6%
Bonds in taxable accounts	+ $0	0%	3.9%	5.2%
	$832,000			

Maximize Utility = $ER - SD^2/RT$, where ER is portfolio after-tax expected returns, SD is portfolio after-tax standard deviation, and RT, the investor's risk tolerance, is set at 0.96. Constraints: $Sr, Br, St, Bt \geq 0$; $Sr + Br = .399$; and $Sr + Br + St + Bt = 1.0$, where Sr denotes the weight of stocks in retirement accounts (i.e. tax-deferred accounts and Roths). Br, St, and Bt denote the weights of bonds in retirement accounts, stocks in taxable accounts, and bonds in taxable accounts. The correlation coefficient between stock and bond returns is 0.2. The active investor pays effective tax rates of 35 percent on bond returns and 15 percent on stock returns. Cost basis of stocks in taxable account is $500,000. Optimization was performed in Excel. TDA denotes tax-deferred accounts such as a 401(k) and Roths denotes tax-exempt accounts such as a Roth IRA.

because bonds and stocks are effectively different assets when held in taxable accounts instead of Roths or tax-deferred accounts.

For example, from this investor's perspective, bonds held in taxable accounts have an after-tax return of 3.9 percent and after-tax risk of 5.2 percent, while the same asset has an after-tax return and risk of 6 percent and 8 percent when held in Roths or tax-deferred accounts. Generalizing, *in an after-tax optimization, the same asset is effectively a different asset when held in 1) a taxable account, 2) a Roth or tax-deferred account, and 3) a non-qualified annuity due to its different risk/reward characteristics.* Moreover, this statement also applies to the recommendations of financial advisers who do not use a formal optimizer. From the individual investor's perspective, the same asset is effectively a different asset when held in 1) a taxable account, 2) a Roth or tax-deferred account, or 3) a non-qualified annuity.

In Table 5.3, the optimal after-tax asset allocation is 39.9 percent bonds and 60.1 percent stocks. The optimal asset location is to hold bonds in Roths and tax-deferred accounts and stocks in taxable accounts, while maintaining the target asset allocation. Unlike the traditional optimization, the after-tax optimization is not silent on the issue of asset location.

To repeat, since the traditional approach is silent on the issue of asset location, it would consider the following portfolio to be optimal: $500,000 in stocks in tax-deferred accounts and tax-exempt Roths and $500,000 in bonds in taxable accounts. Yet, this is dramatically different from the portfolio in Table 5.3.

The traditional approach would also consider the following portfolio to be optimal: $480,000 in bonds in tax-deferred accounts, $20,000 in bonds in Roths, and $500,000 in stocks in taxable accounts. Although this is the same portfolio as in Table 5.3, the traditional approach says this individual has a 50 percent bonds and 50 percent stocks asset mix, while the after-tax approach says he has a 39.9 percent bonds and 60.1 percent stocks mix. The traditional approach overstates the bond exposure and understates the stock exposure by more than 10 percent. Even if a financial adviser using the traditional approach was fortunate enough to locate bonds in tax-exempt Roths and tax-deferred accounts and stocks in taxable accounts, he would have substantially miscalculated the client's asset allocation.

ASSET ALLOCATION VERSUS ASSET LOCATION

Let us return to our hypothetical individual investor who has $312,000 of after-tax funds in tax-deferred accounts, $20,000 in Roths, and $500,000 in taxable accounts. Table 5.3 presented his optimal portfolio for his risk tolerance of 0.96. It holds only bonds in tax-deferred accounts and tax-exempt Roths and only stocks in

taxable accounts. At lower levels of risk tolerance, the optimal portfolio would hold only bonds in tax-deferred accounts and Roths,
but bonds and stocks in taxable accounts. At higher levels of risk
tolerance, it would hold bonds and stocks in tax-deferred accounts
and Roths, but only stocks in taxable accounts. But it would never
hold bonds and stocks in both 1) tax-deferred accounts and Roths
and 2) taxable accounts. (Later, we will discuss an exception to
this rule.) That is, the asset allocation decision takes precedence
over the asset location decision. The allocation of after-tax funds in
tax-deferred accounts and tax-exempt Roths versus taxable accounts
does *not* dictate the asset allocation. Rather, if needed to maintain
the target asset allocation, both bonds and stocks should be held in
tax-deferred accounts and Roths or in taxable accounts.

INTUITIVE EXPLANATION OF ASSET LOCATION

Table 5.4 presents an intuitive explanation of the optimal asset location
decision for this active investor. The left column shows the two asset
location strategies. The first and optimal strategy is to locate 1) bonds
in tax-deferred accounts and Roths and 2) stocks in taxable accounts.
The second strategy is to locate 1) stocks in tax-deferred accounts and

Table 5.4. Optimal Asset Location for Active Stock Investor

Asset Location Strategies	Effective Tax Rates
1. Bonds in tax-deferred accounts and Roths	0%
Stocks in taxable accounts	15%
2. Stocks in tax-deferred accounts and Roths	0%
Bonds in taxable accounts	35%

Roths and 2) bonds in taxable accounts. Because the asset class held in tax-deferred accounts and Roths grows effectively tax exempt, the key issue is whether it is better for this investor to let the government take 15 percent of stocks' returns and risk or 35 percent of bonds' returns and risk when held in taxable accounts. The intuitive answer is that it is better to let the government take 15 percent of stocks returns and risk. Therefore, he should locate stocks in taxable accounts and bonds in tax-deferred accounts and Roths, while maintaining his target asset allocation. Since stocks' returns, but not bonds' returns, receive preferential treatment when held in taxable accounts, it is better to locate stocks in the taxable account.

The intuition presented in Table 5.4 can be extended. It shows that the asset location advantage increases with the spread between the ordinary income tax rate and effective tax rate on stocks when held in taxable accounts, 35 percent – 15 percent in this example. This spread widens with 1) an increase in the ordinary income tax bracket and 2) a decrease in the effective tax rate on stocks held in taxable accounts. As discussed in Chapter 2, the effective tax rate on stocks held in taxable accounts can be reduced by allowing capital gains to grow unharvested, and capital gain taxes can be eliminated by awaiting the step-up in basis at death of donating their appreciated asset to charity. Therefore, the asset location decision should be most important to individuals in high tax brackets who passively manage stocks in their taxable accounts. Many high net worth individuals fit this description. Therefore, the asset location decision should be of special interest to many high net worth individuals.

At the other extreme, the asset location decision would not be important to a day trader who owns only non-dividend paying stocks. Since he would pay ordinary income tax rates on all stock returns, in the example his spread would be 35 percent – 35 percent, or zero. With the exception of this day trader who owns only non-dividend paying stocks, everyone else should have an asset location preference.

OTHER ISSUES

This section examines other issues related to asset location.

Tax-loss Harvesting. The prior analysis examined asset location benefits assuming asset returns are positive. When held in taxable accounts, asset losses can be harvested and used to offset capital gains and reduce taxable income. Since stocks are more volatile than bonds and thus more likely to incur losses, the ability to harvest losses also encourages individuals to hold stocks in taxable accounts and bonds in tax-exempt accounts and tax-deferred accounts.

Tax-exempt Bonds. When presenting this material, a financial adviser may say that he uses tax-exempt bonds in taxable accounts, and ask how this should affect the analysis. Tax-exempt bonds have an implicit tax rate, and this tax rate should be used for the effective tax rate on bonds held in taxable accounts. For example, if taxable bonds selling at par yield 6 percent and otherwise-equivalent tax-exempt bonds selling at par yield 4.5 percent then the effective tax rate is 25 percent. In this case, it would still be preferable to locate taxable bonds in tax-deferred accounts and Roths and stocks in taxable accounts. That is, it is better to let the government take 15 percent of stocks' returns and risk than 25 percent of bonds' returns and risk as would occur if tax-exempt bonds were located in taxable accounts.

Non-qualified Annuities. Table 5.5 extends the analysis to include non-qualified annuities. It summarizes the effective tax rates on bonds and stocks when held in each savings vehicle. Recall that returns in a non-qualified annuity are eventually taxed as ordinary income, even if the underlying asset is stocks producing capital gains. From Table 2.2, assuming an 8 percent annual return all in the form of capital gains, the annuity investor in the 35 percent tax bracket would have to defer gains for about 35 years to reduce the effective tax rate to 15 percent. For the annuity investor in the 25 percent ordinary tax bracket, it would take 19 years to reduce the effective rate to 15 percent. Moreover, the 15 percent tax rate is for an active stock investor. By simply being passive, the effective tax rate on stocks held in taxable accounts is less than 15 percent. This suggests that stocks fare better when held in taxable

Table 5.5. Effective Tax Rates Assuming 35% Ordinary Income Tax Rate and 15% Capital Gain Tax Rate

	Bonds	Stocks
Tax-exempt Roths	0%	0%
Tax-deferred Accounts	0%	0%
Taxable Accounts	35%	35% trader
		15% active investor
		≤15% passive investor
		≈0% exempt investor
Non-qualified Annuities	≤35%	≤35%

accounts than in non-qualified annuities. However, non-qualified variable annuities often have a death benefit that is not present in stock funds held in taxable accounts. This death benefit may help offset the annuity's disadvantage that its returns are eventually taxed as ordinary income. Nevertheless, this analysis suggests that it may be better to hold bonds instead of stocks in annuities, because bonds' interest would be taxed as ordinary income if held in taxable accounts. Further research is needed on this issue.

GUIDE TO ASSET LOCATION

Table 5.6 presents a suggested ordering of assets to be held in 1) tax-deferred accounts and Roths and 2) taxable accounts. The best asset classes to be held in tax-deferred accounts and Roths include:

- Bonds (defined broadly to include all interest-bearing assets, like CDs)
- Real estate investment trusts (REITs), since they generate income that is largely taxed as ordinary income
- Hedge funds, since their returns are generally tax inefficient

After filling tax-deferred accounts and Roths with these assets, the next line of assets for these savings vehicles might be tax-inefficient stock funds, especially active stock funds that tend to distribute short-term capital gains.

Table 5.6: Guide to Asset Location	
Best assets to hold in tax-deferred accounts and tax-exempt Roths:	**Best assets to hold in taxable accounts:**
1. Bonds (defined broadly to include all interest-bearing assets like CDs) 2. Real estate investment trusts (REITs) 3. Hedge funds 4. Tax-inefficient stock funds such as active funds that realize substantial short-term capital gains	1. Stocks or any other asset whose returns will accrue as capital gains and that the individual will let grow unharvested for long horizons. This may include stock index funds, tax-managed stock funds, tax-efficient ETFs, individual stocks, and undeveloped real estate.

If an individual investor has non-qualified annuities, he might place in this savings vehicle whatever else is left after satisfying the location preferences of 1) tax-deferred accounts and Roths and 2) taxable accounts. Because returns are eventually taxed as ordinary income, bonds may be better suited than stocks for non-qualified annuities. Exception: Liquidity or cash reserves are generally held in taxable accounts.

The best asset classes to hold in taxable accounts include any asset whose returns will accrue as capital gains and that the individual will let grow unharvested for long horizons. These may include stock index funds, tax-managed stock funds, tax-efficient ETFs, and individual stocks. Other good choices may include undeveloped real estate. The next choice may be the more tax-efficient stock funds, that is, passive stock funds and active stock funds that distribute little, if any, short-term gains.

If an individual investor has non-qualified annuities, he might place in this savings vehicle whatever else is left after satisfying the location preferences of 1) tax-deferred accounts and Roths and 2) taxable accounts. As mentioned earlier, the tax code encourages holding bonds instead of stocks in non-qualified annuities, but their death benefit would suggest holding stocks in this savings vehicle. I suspect bonds are better suited than stocks to non-qualified annuities, but additional research is needed on this issue.

Exception for Liquidity Reserves. Finally, there is an important exception to the preference order described above and the asset location argument as illustrated in the after-tax optimization. Many retirees prefer to hold liquidity reserves in taxable accounts. It takes about four days to obtain cash from the sale of mutual fund shares held in a tax-deferred account, and this transaction may cause that year's distributions to exceed the required minimum distribution. Consequently, liquidity reserves are generally held in taxable accounts. Therefore, if the individual in the example in this section wants to have $10,000 of liquid reserves in a money market fund then these funds will probably be held in taxable accounts. In Table 5.3, the taxable account would hold $10,000 in money market funds but the remaining $490,000 would be in stocks, preferably passively-managed stocks. This chapter points out that one of the opportunity costs of placing liquidity reserves in taxable accounts is it causes the individual to lose out on the tax code's favorable treatment of stocks when held in taxable accounts.

The next chapter discusses withdrawal strategies during retirement. Suppose a retiree has funds in tax-deferred accounts, tax-exempt accounts, and taxable accounts and she needs $80,000 of after-tax funds for living expenses each year during retirement. Chapter 6 asks and examines what sequence of withdrawals from these savings vehicles will allow her portfolio to last the longest.

SUMMARY

This chapter demonstrated the differences between tax-oblivious mean variance optimization and an after-tax mean variance optimization. In the latter, we 1) adjust assets' market values for embedded tax liabilities and 2) adjust bonds' and stocks' pre-tax returns for taxes when held in taxable accounts. That is, we make adjustments that reflect the reality that taxes exist. Once we make these changes, there is a clear asset location preference. With the exception of liquidity reserves, individuals should locate bonds in tax-deferred accounts and Roths and stocks, especially passively-managed stocks, in taxable accounts, while maintaining their target asset allocation.

The intuitive explanation for this asset location argument is as follows: First, assume returns are positive. The effective tax rates on bonds and stocks are zero when held in tax-deferred accounts and Roths. In contrast, stocks are more favorably taxed than bonds when held in taxable accounts. Therefore, it is better to hold stocks in taxable accounts since the government would take a smaller percentage of stocks' returns and risk than if bonds were held in taxable accounts. If returns are negative, losses on assets held in taxable accounts can be harvested and used to offset capital gains and reduce taxable income. Since stocks are more volatile than bonds, the ability to tax-loss harvest also encourages stocks to be held in taxable accounts.

The asset allocation decision is more important than the asset location decision. Stated differently, the percent of the after-tax portfolio in tax-deferred accounts and Roths versus taxable accounts should not dictate the asset allocation decision. If an individual has 80 percent of his after-tax portfolio in tax-deferred accounts and Roths but wants a 60 percent bonds and 40 percent stocks asset allocation, then he should hold bonds and stocks in tax-deferred accounts and Roths but only stocks in taxable accounts. Finally, we noted that an exception to this asset location preference is that liquidity reserves must be held in taxable account.

For related studies, see Dammon, Spatt, and Zhang (2004) and Reichenstein (2001a and 2007a).

In this chapter, we established the following principles and investment implications.

- When held in taxable accounts, bonds' interest income is taxed at higher effective tax rates than the tax rates on stocks' dividends and long-term capital gains. Therefore, the optimal asset location calls for holding bonds in tax-deferred accounts and Roths and stocks in taxable accounts, while maintaining the target asset allocation.
- An exception to this asset location preference is that liquidity reserves must be held in taxable accounts to serve their purpose.

- In an after-tax mean variance optimization, a bond held in a taxable account is effectively a different asset from the same bond if held in a tax-deferred account or Roth. In general, a stock held in a taxable account is effectively a different asset from the same stock if held in a tax-deferred account or Roth.
- The asset allocation decision is more important than the asset location decision. Therefore, when necessary to maintain the target asset allocation, an individual investor should hold bonds and stocks in either 1) tax-deferred accounts and Roths or 2) taxable accounts. But, with the exception of liquidity reserves, he should not hold bonds and stocks in both 1) tax-deferred accounts and Roths and 2) taxable accounts.

6 Withdrawal Strategies to Make Your Nest Egg Last Longer

Prior chapters established principles and investment implications that are important for individual investors accumulating assets for retirement. This chapter examines investment implications for individuals who are withdrawing funds during retirement. We shall see that principles and investment implications for the accumulation years also have implications for the withdrawal years.

REVIEW

Prior chapters established the following principles and investment implications:

- The *after-tax* value of funds in tax-exempt Roths like the Roth IRA and tax-deferred accounts like the 401(k) grow effectively tax free. (See Chapters 1 and 2.)
- Effective tax rates are higher on assets held in taxable accounts than on assets held in retirement accounts, where retirement accounts include Roths and tax-deferred accounts. (See Chapter 2.)

- The individual investor effectively owns $(1 - t_n)$ of a tax-deferred account's principal, while the government "owns" the other t_n of principal, where t_n is the marginal tax rate when the funds are withdrawn in retirement. (See Chapters 1 and 2.)
- In terms of locating assets between taxable accounts and retirement accounts, when possible while maintaining the desired asset allocation, individuals should place bonds in retirement accounts and stocks, especially passively held stocks, in taxable accounts (with the exception of liquidity reserves, which should be held in taxable accounts). (See Chapter 5.)

These same principles and investment implications also have implications for individuals who are withdrawing assets in their golden years. This chapter guides these individuals' decisions about the optimal sequence for withdrawing funds from savings vehicles during retirement. It is designed to answer questions such as: To maximize a portfolio's longevity—that is, the length of time before it runs out of funds—should a retiree withdraw funds from his taxable account followed by a Roth and then a tax-deferred, or would another withdrawal sequence be preferred? Should the retiree withdraw funds from a Roth and leave funds in the tax-deferred account for a beneficiary or vice versa?

This chapter is adapted from Reichenstein (2006c). It builds on earlier works by Spitzer and Singh (2006), Horan (2006a and 2006b), and my earlier work for TIAA-CREF (see Reichenstein, 2006b, www.tiaa-crefinstitute.org/research/trends). In my earlier works, I considered a retiree who has funds in taxable accounts, tax-deferred accounts, and tax-exempt Roths. In a separate section at the end of this chapter, I extend the analysis to include non-qualified annuities.

WITHDRAWAL STRATEGIES TO MAXIMIZE PORTFOLIO LONGEVITY
In this section, we examine the impact of alternative withdrawal strategies on a portfolio's longevity. Here, we assume that the retiree's goal is to adapt the withdrawal strategy that will maximize

the portfolio's longevity. Therefore, in this section we assume the retiree is not concerned about the amount of funds that will be left for beneficiaries. (Later, we relax this assumption.)

Effective Tax Rates. This section's key principle is: *Effective tax rates are higher on taxable accounts than on retirement accounts, where retirement accounts refers to tax-exempt Roths and tax-deferred accounts.* (Later in this chapter, we extend the analysis to include non-qualified annuities.) Therefore, *as a rule of thumb, retirees should withdraw funds from taxable accounts before retirement accounts.*

Let's consider effective tax rates on bonds and stocks held in each of three savings vehicles: tax-exempt Roths, tax-deferred accounts, and taxable accounts. This chapter will consider a lower-wealth retiree, who will be in the 15 percent ordinary income and 5 percent capital gains tax brackets, and a higher-wealth retiree, who will be in the 25 percent ordinary income and 15 percent capital gain brackets. Many individuals will be in higher tax brackets, especially when state taxes are considered. As will become clear, the withdrawal sequence should be even more important to these investors.

Table 6.1 presents the lower-wealth and higher-wealth retirees' effective tax rates on bonds and stocks when held in each of three savings vehicles.

Table 6.1. Effective Tax Rates on Assets Held in Tax-exempt Roths, Tax-deferred Accounts, and Taxable Accounts

	Lower-Wealth Retirees		Higher-Wealth Retirees	
	Bonds	**Stocks**	**Bonds**	**Stocks**
Tax-exempt Roths	0%	0%	0%	0%
Tax-deferred Accounts	0%	0%	0%	0%
Taxable Accounts	15%	5%	25%	15%

Tax-exempt Roths include Roth IRA, Roth 401(k), and Roth 403(b), while tax-deferred accounts include traditional IRA, 401(k), 403(b), 457, SEP-IRA, and Keogh plans.

The effective tax rate on bonds and stocks held in Roths is zero. The funds grow tax exempt, assuming the withdrawal occurs after age 59½ and the account has been in existence for at least five years. As explained in Chapters 1 and 2, the *after-tax* value of funds held in tax-deferred accounts also grows effectively tax exempt; the effective tax rate is zero.

When held in taxable accounts, individuals pay taxes each year on bond's interest income at the ordinary income tax rate. Since capital gains tend to be negligible on bonds, the effective tax rate on bonds held in taxable accounts is 15 percent for the lower-wealth couple and 25 percent for the higher-wealth couple.

As explained in Chapter 2, the effective tax rate on stocks held in taxable accounts depends, in part, on when the investor realizes capital gains. This chapter's models assume the stock investors are active investors who realize all gains each year—technically in one year and one day. They pay taxes each year on qualified dividends and capital gains at the long-term capital gains rate. The effective tax rate for the lower-wealth couple is 5 percent and the effective rate for the higher-wealth couple is 15 percent. Later in this chapter, we will consider 1) passive investors who allow gains to grow unrealized for several years but eventually pay taxes on the gains and 2) exempt investors who avoid taxes by either awaiting the step-up in basis at death or donating the appreciated stock to a qualified charity.

Table 6.1 summarizes the effective tax rates for lower-wealth and higher-wealth retired couples who are active stock investors. Since they pay higher effective tax rates on assets held in taxable accounts, they should withdraw funds from taxable accounts before retirement accounts.

Withdrawal Strategies and Longevity. The intuition from Table 6.1 is that a strategy of withdrawing funds from taxable accounts before retirement accounts should allow the portfolio to last longer than a strategy of withdrawing funds from retirement accounts before taxable accounts. This section is designed to provide insights into the additional longevity from following this preferred strategy.

To estimate the additional longevity, we examine detailed models that provide reasonable estimates of the additional longevity provided by withdrawing funds from taxable accounts first. In addition, they provide insights about when retirees should deviate from this rule of thumb.

The models provide insight into the likely additional portfolio longevity from the strategy of withdrawing funds from taxable accounts before retirement accounts instead of withdrawing funds in the opposite order. Although defined in detail later, we refer to the strategy of withdrawing funds from taxable accounts before retirement accounts as the Taxable Accounts First strategy. We call the strategy of withdrawing funds from retirement accounts before taxable accounts the Retirement Accounts First strategy. The models are designed to be forward looking. They use key features of the tax code including the 2005 tax brackets, and assume future bond returns that are consistent with then-current yields. Of course, stock returns are more difficult to predict. To provide some range of possible returns, the models assumed the next 30 years will repeat either 1973–2002 returns on the S&P 500—henceforth, the poor returns sequence—or 1976–2005 returns—henceforth, the good returns sequence. Due to the 1973–1974 stock losses, which were similar to 2000–2002 inflation-adjusted losses on the S&P 500, the 1973–2002 withdrawal period proved especially difficult for retirees. Withdrawal rate studies generally conclude that individuals who began retirement in 1973 were able to withdraw the least amount from their portfolios and still have their portfolios last a given number of years. Thus we intentionally chose to use this poor returns sequence. But we also used the good returns sequence.

There are separate models for lower-wealth and higher-wealth retired couples. Each couple is 66 years old. The lower-wealth couple has a $1 million after-tax portfolio consisting of $100,000 in a Roth, $300,000 in taxable accounts, and $600,000 of after-tax funds in tax-deferred accounts. Based on today's tax code, they will usually be in the 15 percent ordinary income tax bracket and

5 percent capital gain bracket during retirement. So the $600,000 of after-tax funds in the tax-deferred account is equivalent to $705,882 of pre-tax funds, [$600,000/(1 − 0.15)].

The higher wealth couple has a $2 million after-tax portfolio consisting of $200,000 in Roths, $1 million of after-tax funds in tax-deferred accounts, and $800,000 in taxable accounts.

Each couple's objective is to withdraw the largest constant real (or inflation adjusted) amount each year such that the portfolio lasts 30 years. Although their joint life expectancy is less than 30 years, they plan for a 30-year horizon to provide reasonable assurance that their portfolio will last throughout their lives.

We modeled two withdrawal strategies:

- **The Taxable Accounts First Strategy:** In this strategy, the couple withdraws funds in the following order: 1) required minimum distributions (RMDs), when applicable, from tax-deferred accounts, 2) bonds and then stocks held in taxable accounts, 3) stocks and then bonds held in Roths, and 4) stocks and then bonds held in tax-deferred accounts.
- **The Retirement Accounts First Strategy:** In this strategy, the couple withdraws funds in the following order: 1) RMDs, when applicable, from tax-deferred accounts, 2) stocks and then bonds held in Roths, 3) stocks and then bonds held in tax-deferred accounts, and 4) bonds and then stocks held in taxable accounts.

Required minimum distributions are assumed to begin when the couple is age 70. Adopting the asset-location advice discussed in Chapter 5, we assumed stocks were held in taxable accounts and bonds in retirement accounts to the degree possible while maintaining the 50 percent stocks and 50 percent bonds target asset allocation.

After each beginning-of-year distribution, the portfolios were rebalanced back to a 50 percent stocks and 50 percent bonds after-tax asset allocation. Thus, differences in longevity are due to differences in effective tax rates and not to differences in asset allocation. For other model details, see a special section titled "The Model's Assumptions," at the end of this chapter.

Table 6.2 presents results for both couples and the two 30-year returns sequences.

Table 6.2. Additional Longevity from Taxable Accounts First Strategy Compared to Retirement Accounts First Strategy				
Lower-Wealth Retirees		Portfolio Longevities (years)		
Returns Sequence	Initial Withdrawal	Taxable Accounts First	Retirement Accounts First	Additional Longevity
Poor	$34,949	30.0	27.7	2.3
Good	$48,908	30.0	27.6	2.4
Poor	$50,000	16.5	16.0	0.5
Good	$50,000	28.6	26.5	2.1
Higher-Wealth Retirees		Portfolio Longevities (years)		
Returns Sequence	Initial Withdrawal	Taxable Accounts First	Retirement Accounts First	Additional Longevity
Poor	$73,364	30.0	24.6	5.4
Good	$98,734	30.0	24.7	5.3
Poor	$100,000	17.4	16.2	1.2
Good	$100,000	29.3	24.1	5.2

First, let's consider the lower-wealth couple. With the poor returns sequence, if this couple followed the Taxable Accounts First strategy, they could withdraw $34,949 in 2005, the first retirement year, and an inflation-adjusted equivalent amount each year thereafter, and the portfolio would last precisely 30 years. If they withdrew the same amount using the Retirement Accounts First strategy, the portfolio would last 27.7 years. Therefore, the portfolio's longevity was 2.3 years longer with the Taxable Accounts First strategy.

With the good returns sequence, the couple could withdraw $48,908 in 2005, the first retirement year, and an inflation-adjusted equivalent amount each year thereafter and the portfolio would last precisely 30 years. If they withdrew the same amount using the Retirement Accounts First strategy, the portfolio would last 27.6

years. Therefore, the portfolio's longevity was 2.4 years longer with the Taxable Accounts First strategy.

The longevity advantage is generally shorter when the initial withdrawal is larger. For example, if the initial withdrawal is $50,000, then the additional longevity from the Taxable Accounts First strategy is 0.5 years for the poor returns sequence and 2.1 years for the good returns sequence.

In sum, the lower-wealth couple may be able to lengthen the portfolio's longevity by perhaps two years by following the Taxable Accounts First strategy instead of the Retirement Accounts First strategy. The higher-wealth couple pays higher effective tax rates on bonds and stock held in taxable accounts. Therefore, it follows that the additional portfolio longevity from following the Taxable Accounts First strategy should be larger for this couple.

With the poor returns sequence and an initial withdrawal of $73,364, the Taxable Accounts First strategy lasts 30 years and the Retirement Accounts First strategy lasted 24.6 years. The additional longevity is 5.4 years. With the good returns sequence and an initial withdrawal of $98,734, the additional longevity is 5.3 years.

As before, the longevity advantage is generally shorter when the initial withdrawal is larger. For an initial withdrawal of $100,000, the additional longevity from the Taxable Accounts First strategy is 1.2 years for the poor returns sequence and 5.2 years for the good returns sequence.

In short, due to the higher effective tax rates in taxable accounts, the higher-wealth couple may be able to lengthen the portfolios' longevity by about five years by following the Taxable Accounts First strategy.

The Problem of Uncertainty. Table 6.3 succinctly illustrates the difficult task facing retirees and the importance of two uncertainties: the length of remaining life and future returns. For a 30-year lifespan and the poor returns sequence, the portfolio would only support a 3.5 percent initial withdrawal rate. For a 30-year lifespan and the good returns sequence, the portfolio would support an initial withdrawal rate of 4.9 percent.

Table 6.3. Largest Sustainable Initial After-tax Withdrawal Rates by Portfolio Longevity and Time Period		
Portfolio Longevity		
Returns Sequence	**20-Year**	**30-Year**
Poor	4.4%	3.5%
Good	6.0%	4.9%

These sustainable initial withdrawal rates are for the lower-wealth retired couple.

For a 20-year lifespan, the initial withdraw rates are about 1 percent higher for both the poor and good returns sequences. These results illustrate the problem facing retirees. Since they do not know how long they will live or whether future stock returns will be strong or weak, the conservative strategy is to plan for a long lifespan and poor returns.

The models confirm the intuition as expressed in the rule of thumb: *In general, retirees should withdraw funds from taxable accounts before retirement accounts.* Moreover, the higher the retiree's effective tax rates on assets held in taxable accounts, the larger is the additional portfolio longevity from following this withdrawal sequence. Therefore, if Congress raises U.S. tax rates then the longevity advantage from following the Taxable Accounts First strategy should lengthen.

Exceptions to the Rule of Thumb. This section discusses exceptions to the rule of thumb to withdraw funds from taxable accounts before retirement accounts.

The first exception occurs for retirees who will be in an unusually low tax bracket in years before required minimum distributions (RMDs) begin. RMDs begin after age 70½. Before this time, a retired couple or single retiree who is withdrawing funds from taxable accounts may have minimal "taxable income." ("Taxable income" refers to the tax term. That is, it is Adjusted Gross Income less standard or itemized deductions and other deductions such as for personal exemptions.) Withdrawals from taxable accounts are largely, if not entirely, a return of principal. They provide cash to live on, but these transactions usually produce negligible taxable income. For example, a withdrawal from a bank savings account provides cash to live on, but it is not taxable income. Thus retirees who have quit work and are living off funds withdrawn from taxable accounts will frequently have minimal taxable income before RMDs begin.

In these usually low tax rate years, retirees should either withdraw sufficient funds from tax-deferred accounts to fully use low tax brackets, or convert sufficient funds from tax-deferred accounts to Roth IRAs to fully use the low brackets.

For example, suppose the lower-wealth couple earned $18,400 in wages in 2005. For this couple, in 2005, the sum of standard deduction, two deductions for personal exemptions, plus $1,000 deduction each for being over age 65, totaled $18,400. So, after these deductions, this couple's taxable income was zero.

Since the first $14,000 of taxable income in 2005 was taxed at 10 percent, this couple should have either withdrawn $14,000 from a tax-deferred account or converted $14,000 from a traditional IRA to a Roth IRA to fully use the 10 percent tax bracket.

Similarly, the higher-wealth couple should make sure they fully use the 10 percent and 15 percent tax brackets. In 2005, the top of the 15 percent tax bracket was $59,400 of taxable income. These retirees should not waste the opportunity to withdraw funds from tax-deferred accounts when they would be subject to unusually low tax rates.

A second exception occurs for an exempt investor (as described in Chapter 2) who will avoid capital gain taxes on appreciated stocks held in taxable accounts. In essence, the effective tax rate on these capital gains is zero, but only if the retiree awaits the step up in basis at death or donates the appreciated stock to a qualified charity.

To illustrate the logic, assume a single retiree is terminally ill and has a short life expectancy. After his death, his beneficiary will inherit the stock with the cost basis stepped up to the market value at the time of his death. It would be foolish for the retiree to sell the stock and thus pay taxes on the realized capital gains.[1] Similarly, if he will donate the appreciated stock to a qualified charity, the capital gain taxes will be avoided due to the charity's tax-exempt status.

In these cases, he should not follow the rule of thumb. Instead, he should obtain funds from other sources including, if necessary, withdrawing funds from retirement accounts.

Let's change the example to a passive investor who holds appreciated stocks in taxable accounts. He should liquidate the appreciated stock before withdrawing funds from retirement accounts. Since he is a passive investor, the gains will be tax-deferred, potentially for many years, so the effective tax rate on the stocks will be less than the long-term capital gain tax rate. For the lower-wealth couple, the effective rate will be less than 5 percent, and for the higher-wealth couple, it will be less than 15 percent. However, the effective tax rate will still be positive. And, intuitively, it is better for this passive investor to withdraw funds from taxable accounts, where returns are taxed at positive effective rates, than to withdraw funds from retirement accounts, where returns grow effectively tax exempt. Therefore, if a passive investor has an appreciated asset held in a taxable account on which he expects to eventually pay taxes, then he should sell this asset before liquidating retirement accounts.

WITHDRAWAL STRATEGIES FROM RETIREMENT ACCOUNTS

The prior section established the rule of thumb to liquidate taxable assets before retirement assets. This section considers whether retirees should withdraw funds from Roths before tax-deferred accounts or vice versa.

The key principle in this section is: *The individual investor effectively owns $(1 - t_n)$ of a tax-deferred account's principal, while the* government "owns" the other t_n of principal, where t_n is the marginal tax rate when the funds are withdrawn in retirement. The idea is to minimize t_n, the government's share of the tax-deferred account's principal.

To minimize the government's share of the tax-deferred account's principal, funds should be withdrawn from tax-deferred accounts whenever the retiree is in an unusually low tax bracket. Three situations where taxable income might be unusually low include:

1. Years before required minimum distributions begin (as discussed previously)
2. Years with large charitable contributions
3. Years with large deductible medical expenses

Suppose a retiree makes a large charitable contribution out of taxable accounts. This contribution would increase itemized deductions (subject to income limits affecting the maximum deductible contribution), which may result in a low level of taxable income.

Separately, special pension legislation allowed opportunities for individuals over age 70½ to donate funds out of tax-deferred accounts. For tax years 2006 and 2007, individuals over 70½ could move up to $100,000 out of their traditional IRAs directly to a qualified charity. This donation would not affect their taxable income, and the contribution would count toward that year's RMD. Congress is considering reintroducing such opportunities in the future.

Finally, retirees may be in a low tax rate in a year that they have large deductible medical expenses. Medical expenses are deductible to the degree that they exceed 7.5 percent of Adjusted Gross Income. Medical expenses may include all costs associated with full nursing home care and most costs associated with assisted living and independent living arrangements. It is often difficult for a retiree to predict whether she will have large medical expenses, since these expenses tend to occur late in life. Nevertheless, retirees who suspect that they will have large medical expenses might save tax-deferred accounts for those years.

This chapter builds on prior studies on the withdrawal sequence in retirement. In what may be the first study, Spitzer and Singh (2006) report the "surprising" and "counter-intuitive" conclusion that in the presence of a flat tax rate, "it does not matter in which order withdrawals are taken from a tax-deferred or tax-exempt account, all else being equal." That is, retirees should be indifferent between withdrawing funds from tax-exempt Roths and then tax-deferred accounts or tax-deferred accounts and then tax-exempt Roths. This conclusion follows directly from the ideas that $1 in a tax-deferred account is like $(1 - t_n)$ dollar in a Roth and the investor owns $(1 - t_n)$ of the tax-deferred account's principal, but receives all returns and bears all risk.

Horan (2006a and 2006b) contributed to this literature by considering the optimal withdrawal procedure in the presence of a progressive tax rate system. In his study, the individual had funds in Roths and tax-deferred accounts. Like this book, he emphasizes that a dollar in a tax-deferred account is like $(1 - t_n)$ dollar in a Roth. In a progressive tax rate system, he advocates a strategy of withdrawing funds from tax-deferred accounts to use low marginal brackets and then withdrawing additional funds from Roths. His strategy follows directly from the idea that the government owns t_n of the tax-deferred account's principal, so the individual should withdraw funds from these accounts whenever t_n is low.

Retiree Versus Beneficiary's Tax Rates. One additional consideration for a retiree who wants to bequeath funds is the relationship between her marginal tax rate and the marginal tax rate of her beneficiary. Everything else the same, if the retiree has a higher tax rate than the beneficiary, she should withdraw funds from the Roth and leave funds from the tax-deferred account for the beneficiary.

For example, if the retiree has a 25 percent tax rate and the individual beneficiary has a 15 percent tax rate, then $100 in a tax-deferred account would be worth $75 after taxes to the retiree, but $85 to the beneficiary. If the beneficiary is a charity, then the $100 would be worth $75 after taxes to the retiree, but $100 to the charity. So, a retiree who plans to bequeath, say, $100,000 to a charity should retain $100,000 in tax-deferred accounts and designate these assets to the charity.

Everything else the same, if the retiree has a lower tax rate than the beneficiary, she should withdraw funds from the tax-deferred account and leave funds from the Roth for the beneficiary. For example, if the retiree has a 10 percent tax rate and the individual beneficiary has a 25 percent rate, then $100 in a tax-deferred account would be worth $90 after taxes to the retiree, but only $75 to the beneficiary.

EXTENDING THE ANALYSIS TO INCLUDE NON-QUALIFIED ANNUITIES

This section extends the analysis in this chapter to include non-qualified annuities. As we shall see, there are some complexities associated with annuities that are better handled in a separate section. Moreover, since most individuals do not have annuities, it is useful to separate these complexities from the heart of the chapter.

Table 6.4 presents the effective tax rates on bonds and stocks when held in each of four savings vehicles: tax-exempt Roths, tax-deferred accounts, taxable accounts, and non-qualified annuities. For stocks held in taxable accounts, Table 6.4 assumes the individual is an active investor. Since we previously discussed the effective tax rates for Roths, tax-deferred accounts, and taxable accounts, we limit discussion here to non-qualified annuities. Returns on an annuity grow tax-deferred until withdrawal but are eventually taxed as ordinary income. Whether the underlying asset is bonds or stocks, the returns are eventually taxed at 15 percent for the lower-income couple and 25 percent for the higher-income couple. Table 6.4 assumes the funds remain in an annuity for more than one year, so the effective tax rates are less than 15 percent and less than 25 percent for these couples. Table 2.2 showed that these effective tax rates decrease as the investment horizon lengthens.

Table 6.4. Effective Tax Rates on Assets Held in Tax-exempt Roths, Tax-deferred Accounts, Taxable Accounts, and Non-qualified Annuities for Multi-year Horizons				
	Lower-Wealth Retirees		Higher-Wealth Retirees	
	Bonds	Stocks	Bonds	Stocks
Tax-exempt Roths	0%	0%	0%	0%
Tax-deferred Accounts	0%	0%	0%	0%
Taxable Accounts	15%	5%	25%	15%
Non-qualified Annuities	<15%	<15%	<25%	<25%

Tax-exempt Roths include Roth IRA, Roth 401(k), and Roth 403(b), while tax-deferred accounts include traditional IRA, 401(k), 403(b), 457, SEP-IRA, and Keogh plans. Stocks held in taxable accounts are assumed to be held by active investors as defined in Chapter 2.

The rule of thumb is the same as in the Taxable Account First strategy: The retiree should withdraw funds from the most highly taxed savings vehicle first, the second most highly taxed savings vehicle second, and so on. If the underlying asset is bonds, this rule of thumb suggests that funds should be withdrawn from the taxable account first, the non-qualified annuity second, and the Roths and tax-deferred accounts last. If the underlying asset is stocks, it suggests that funds should be withdrawn from the non-qualified annuity and taxable account first, but the order between these two savings vehicles depends upon the length of the investment horizon. For the lower-income couple, Table 2.2 suggests that it takes about 40 years for the benefit of tax-deferred growth to lower their effective tax rate on stocks held in an annuity from 15 percent to 5 percent. For the higher-income couple, it takes about 20 years for the benefit of tax-deferred growth to lower their effective tax rate on stocks held in an annuity from 25 percent to 15 percent. This suggests that most investors pay a higher effective tax rate on stocks held in annuities than on stocks held in taxable accounts. Therefore, the tax code suggests that if the withdrawal will come from bonds, the withdrawal sequence should be taxable accounts, non-qualified annuities, and then Roths and tax-deferred accounts. In general, if the withdrawal will come from stocks, the withdrawal sequence should be non-qualified annuities, taxable accounts, and then Roths and tax-deferred accounts.

Although I believe these rules of thumb are useful guidelines, they should be applied with recognition of unique features of annuities and, to a lesser extent, taxable accounts. Some of these unique features and their consequences are discussed below.

First, the above analysis implicitly assumed that the underlying net return on bonds and stocks is the same, no matter which savings vehicle they are held in. Since the same bond and stock funds can be held in taxable accounts, Roths, and tax-deferred accounts, that is a reasonable assumption for these savings vehicles. But most annuities charge substantially higher annual fees than those charged by the average bond and stock funds. Since the average investor in an annuity may pay 1.25 percent per year more than the average investor in a mutual fund, he will earn a commensurately lower net return. Although there are a few low-cost annuities, most charge much higher expenses. Table 6.4 correctly notes that the tax code favors holding bonds in an annuity instead of a taxable account, but it does not consider the higher costs on most annuities. Suppose the annuity charges 1 percent higher expenses and bonds' gross returns are 6 percent. This 1 percent higher expense and thus 1 percent lower net return is like the investor paying a 16.7 percent higher annual tax rate. Everything else the same, these higher expenses would suggest withdrawing funds from annuities as soon as possible.

Second, most annuities charge surrender fees on withdrawals before the end of a surrender period. Unfortunately, this may limit the speed with which funds should be withdrawn from the annuity. To be more exact, annuities usually allow withdrawals of up to 10 percent of the account's value per year (or sometimes up to 10 percent of original principal per year) with no penalty fee, but they charge a penalty fee on additional withdrawals in any year before the end of the surrender period. The surrender period typically lasts about seven years. Obviously, the existence of a surrender fee may affect the preference for withdrawing funds from an annuity or, at least, the preference for withdrawing funds beyond the 10 percent limit.

Third, annuities usually have a death benefit. One common death benefit promises the individual that, at death, the beneficiary will receive the larger of 1) the annuity's then-current account value or 2) the original principal (less prior withdrawals). This feature reduces the risk of the underlying asset that is borne by the investor/beneficiary. Everything else the same, this death benefit suggests holding stocks in annuities, because they are more volatile than bonds. But, as we have seen, the fact that stock returns are eventually taxed as ordinary income discourages individuals from holding stocks in annuities. So, there is a tradeoff. However, the following example shows that the relationship between the account value and original principal affects the value of the death benefit and should influence the preference order of withdrawals.

Suppose that several years ago, Joe invested $100,000 in an annuity and he has made no withdrawals. At his death, his beneficiary will receive the larger of $100,000 or the then-current account value. If the annuity's account value today is less than $100,000—say, it is $80,000—then Joe will likely withdraw funds from taxable accounts before the annuity. By retaining the annuity, if Joe died today, his beneficiary would receive $100,000, or $20,000 more than the account value.

On the other hand, if the annuity's current market value substantially exceeds $100,000—say, it is $150,000—then the death benefit has negligible value since there is negligible chance that the account value would fall below $100,000. So Joe could ignore the death benefit and would likely withdraw funds from the annuity before taxable accounts.

Finally, there are valuable tax options on assets held in taxable accounts. When held in taxable accounts, individuals: 1) can harvest tax losses, 2) have the potential to avoid capital gains taxes by either awaiting the step-up in basis or donating the appreciated asset to charity, and 3) can use foreign tax credits to reduce taxes. These opportunities are seldom available on assets held in non-qualified annuities.[2] Everything else the same, they encourage individuals to withdraw funds from non-qualified annuities before taxable accounts. Table 6.4 ignores these features of the tax code.

In summary, as a rule of thumb, funds should be withdrawn from taxable accounts and non-qualified annuities first, while funds should be retained until last in Roths and tax-deferred accounts. The preference order for withdrawing funds from taxable accounts and non-qualified annuities depends upon several factors including a) whether the underlying asset is bonds or stocks; b) the additional costs of the annuities; c) the annuities' surrender penalties; and d) whether the annuities' death benefit exceeds its current market value.

The next chapter presents a brief summary of the major points and investment implications of each chapter. In addition, it recommends readings that cover trust-related issues that may be of special interest to advisers of high net worth clients.

SUMMARY

The tax-based withdrawal strategies revolve around two key principles:

First, returns are taxed more heavily in taxable accounts than retirement accounts—that is, tax-exempt Roths and tax-deferred accounts such as 401(k)s. Therefore, as a rule of thumb, retirees should withdraw funds from taxable accounts before retirement accounts. Detailed models suggest that following this rule of thumb may allow a retiree's portfolio to last perhaps two to five years longer, depending upon his or her level of wealth and tax rates.

However, there are exceptions to this rule of thumb. First, before the retiree begins required minimum distributions (RMDs), if her taxable income is unusually low then she should either withdraw sufficient funds from tax-deferred accounts or convert sufficient funds from traditional IRAs to Roth IRAs to fully use low tax brackets. Second, if the retiree has substantial unrealized capital gains on assets held in taxable accounts and will await the step up in basis at death or donate the appreciated asset to charity, then she should withdraw funds from retirement accounts before liquidating the appreciated asset.

A separate section at the end of the chapter extends the analysis to include non-qualified annuities. The same principle applies: As a rule of thumb, retirees should withdraw funds from the most highly taxed savings vehicle first, the second most highly taxed savings vehicle second, and so on. As a rule of thumb, funds should be withdrawn from taxable accounts and non-qualified annuities first, while funds should be retained until last in Roths and tax-deferred accounts.

The second key principle is that the investor effectively owns $(1 - t_n)$ of tax-deferred accounts' principal, while the government effectively owns the remaining t_n of principal. The objective is to minimize the government's share. To do this, the retiree should withdraw funds from tax-deferred accounts whenever she is in a year with an unusually low tax rate. Such years are likely to occur: 1) before RMDs begin, 2) in years when the retiree makes a large contribution, and 3) in years when there are large deductible medical expenses.

Finally, the relationship between the retiree's and beneficiary's marginal tax rates could influence the retiree's decision to withdraw funds from tax-deferred accounts before Roths or vice versa. Everything else the same, if the retiree's tax rate exceeds the beneficiary's then the retiree should withdraw funds from Roths and leave the tax-deferred accounts' balances to the beneficiary. If the retiree's tax bracket is lower than the beneficiary's, then she should withdraw funds from tax-deferred accounts and leave the Roths' balances to the beneficiary.

In this chapter, we established the following principles and investment implications.

- Returns are taxed more heavily in taxable accounts than retirement accounts—that is, tax-exempt Roths and tax-deferred accounts. Therefore, as a rule of thumb, retirees should withdraw funds from taxable accounts before these retirement accounts.
- There are two exceptions to this rule of thumb. First, before required minimum distributions (RMDs) begin, if the retiree's taxable income is unusually low then she should either withdraw sufficient funds from tax-deferred accounts or convert sufficient funds from traditional IRAs to Roth IRAs to fully use low tax brackets. Second, if the retiree has unrealized capital gains on assets held in taxable accounts and will await the step up in basis at death or donate the appreciated asset to charity then she should withdraw funds from retirement accounts before liquidating the appreciated asset.
- Funds in non-qualified annuities are taxed more heavily than funds in Roths and tax-deferred accounts. Therefore, as a rule of thumb, funds should be withdrawn from taxable accounts and non-qualified annuities before Roths and tax-deferred accounts.
- The second key principle is that the government effectively owns t_n of tax-deferred accounts' principal. The objective is to minimize t_n. To the degree possible, withdrawals from tax-deferred accounts should be timed for low tax rate years such as: 1) before RMDs begin, 2) in years when the retiree makes a large contribution, and 3) in years when there are large deductible medical expenses.
- In general, if the retiree's marginal tax rate exceeds the beneficiary's then the retiree should withdraw funds from Roths and leave the tax-deferred accounts' balances to the beneficiary, and vice versa.

ENDNOTES

[1] See Chapters 2 and 3 for further discussion of the step up in basis and charitable donations.

[2] Annuity losses can be deducted against ordinary income as miscellaneous itemized deductions. Therefore, to use them the individual must 1) itemize deductions and 2) miscellaneous itemized deductions must exceed 2% of Adjusted Gross Income. In practice, these criteria are seldom met.

THE MODELS' ASSUMPTIONS

The objective of the models is to estimate how much longer retirees' portfolios might last if they withdraw funds from taxable accounts before retirement accounts instead of the opposite strategy. That is, what is the additional portfolio longevity from following the Taxable Accounts First strategy instead of the Retirement Accounts First strategy?

To answer this question, we modeled key features of the 2005 tax code and potential future returns on bonds and stocks. We calculated the largest real (that is, inflation-adjusted) after-tax withdrawal that the couple could make each year following the Taxable Accounts First strategy and still have the portfolio survive for 30 years. We then calculated the portfolio's longevity for this annual withdrawal amount when following the Retirement Accounts First strategy. The difference is an estimate of the additional longevity from following the Taxable Accounts First strategy.

The models assume the retired couple has no earned income (for example, wages and salaries) during retirement. The couple makes required minimum distributions from tax-deferred accounts each year, and the first required distribution occurs in the calendar year the couple turns 70. Additional distributions to maintain their annual after-tax withdrawal amount come from taxable accounts or retirement accounts, where the latter may include additional withdrawals from tax-deferred accounts. Their taxable income consists of all distributions from tax-deferred accounts.

Gross bond returns are assumed to be 5 percent, which was consistent with long-term Treasury yields at the time of this study. Of course, gross stock returns are more difficult to predict. To provide some range of possible returns, we assumed the next 30 years will repeat either 1973–2002 returns on the S&P 500—a poor returns sequence—or 1976–2005 returns—a good returns sequence.

Net bond and stock returns are set 1 percent per year lower than the gross returns to reflect financial planner's fees, mutual funds' expense ratios and transaction costs. For simplicity, the models assume all capital gains and losses are realized each year—technically, in one year and one day. So all stock returns are taxable each year at the long-term gains tax rate. Consistent with mutual fund distribution requirements, the models assume net losses cannot be passed through to investors, but are accumulated and used to offset future capital gains. Taxes on net realized capital gains are paid each year.

The models assume the first withdrawal in retirement occurs in 2005. In 2005, the first $14,000 of taxable income for a couple filing jointly was taxed at 10 percent, taxable income up to $59,400 was taxed at 15 percent, and so on. These brackets increased each year with inflation as measured by the Consumer Price Index. Adopting the asset location advice from Chapter 5, we assumed stocks were held in taxable accounts and bonds in retirement accounts to the degree possible while maintaining the 50 percent stocks and 50 percent bonds target asset allocation. After each beginning-of-year distribution, the portfolios were rebalanced to a 50 percent stocks and 50 percent bonds after-tax asset allocation.

In the base case, the 66-year-old retired couple has a $1 million after-tax portfolio. They have $100,000 in a tax-exempt account, $300,000 in taxable accounts, and $600,000 of after-tax funds in tax-deferred accounts. Assuming stock returns and inflation rates will repeat the poor sequence, the portfolio would support an after-tax withdrawal of $34,949 per year, an inflation-adjusted equivalent amount each year thereafter, and would be exhausted after 30 years.

In other simulations, I insert one or more of the following assumptions: 1) future stock returns and inflation rates will repeat the good sequence, 2) the initial after-tax portfolio contains $2 million, consisting of $800,000 in taxable accounts, $200,000 in tax-exempt Roths, and $1 million of after-tax funds in tax-deferred accounts, and 3) a different initial withdrawal amount.

Although the models' basic assumptions precisely fit few retirees, I am confident that the models provide useful estimates of the sensitivity of the portfolios' longevity to alternative withdrawal strategies.

7 | *Summary and More*

By design, this book was limited to a discussion of the after-tax valuation of assets held in one of four savings vehicles: tax-exempt accounts such as Roth IRAs, tax-deferred accounts such as 401(k)s, taxable accounts, and non-qualified tax-deferred annuities. As discussed in Appendix A, there is broad agreement among scholars about how we should calculate the after-tax value of assets held in tax-deferred accounts. In particular, and as explained in Chapter 1, each dollar in a tax-deferred account is like $(1 - t_n)$ dollar of after-tax funds in a tax-exempt Roth, where t_n is the marginal tax rate in retirement. For example, for someone who will have a 25 percent tax rate in retirement, each dollar in a tax-deferred account is like $0.75 in a Roth because they will each buy the same amount of goods and services in retirement. Conceptually, each pre-tax dollar in a tax-deferred account can be separated into $(1 - t_n)$ dollar of the individual investor's after-tax funds plus t_n, the government's share of the current principal.

Chapter 2 showed how the choice of savings vehicles affects the percent of principal effectively owned by, the percent of return received by, and the percent of risk borne by individual investors. It showed that the *after-tax* value of funds in tax-deferred accounts grows effectively tax exempt. Continuing with the prior example, for each dollar of pre-tax funds in a tax-deferred account, $0.75 is the investor's after-tax funds. The after-tax value of these funds grows from $0.75 today to $0.75(1 + r)^n$, where r is the pre-tax rate of return and n is the length of the investment horizon. So, the after-tax value grows effectively tax exempt. For assets held in tax-deferred accounts and Roths, the investor receives all returns and bears all risk. For bonds held in taxable accounts, the investor receives about $(1 - t)$ of returns and bears about $(1 - t)$ of risk, where t is the marginal tax rate on ordinary income. For stocks held in taxable accounts, the percent of returns received by and risk borne by the investor varies with the stock management style. For an active investor who realizes all gains after a year and a day, the percent is about $(1 - t_c)$, where t_c is the preferential tax rate on capital gains and qualified dividends.

To repeat, Chapters 1 and 2 established that each dollar in a tax-deferred account should be viewed as $(1 - t_n)$ dollar in a Roth. This concept has important investment implications for the:

1. Calculation of an individual's after-tax asset allocation
2. Asset location decision
3. Preferential withdrawal sequence from savings vehicles in retirement

These issues are the topics of Chapters 3, 5, and 6.

Chapter 3 explains how financial advisers should calculate individuals' after-tax asset allocations. To calculate an after-tax asset allocation, we must convert assets' market values to after-tax values by adjusting their market values for embedded tax liabilities. We then calculate the asset allocation using these after-tax values. For most individuals, the largest adjustment by far is the conversion of their tax-deferred accounts' pre-tax values for embedded tax liabilities.

Chapter 4 examined the choice of savings vehicles for someone who is saving for retirement. For example, when given a choice, should someone save in a 401(k) or Roth 401(k)? A key factor in this decision is a comparison between the marginal tax rate in the contribution year, t, and the marginal tax rate in the withdrawal year, t_n. In general, when the retirement tax rate is less than the current tax rate (that is, $t_n < t$), the individual should save in a tax-deferred account before a Roth, and vice versa. When the two rates are the same or even close, other factors may play a deciding role. Most of these other factors favor saving in Roths before tax-deferred accounts. They include: 1) the maximum annual contribution is effectively larger when it is made with after-tax dollars instead of pre-tax dollars, 2) the lack of effective required minimum distributions on Roths,[1] and 3) distributions from tax-deferred accounts may increase taxes on Social Security benefits (as discussed in Appendix B).

Chapter 5 compared a tax-oblivious traditional mean variance optimization with a tax-aware after-tax mean variance optimization. The after-tax optimization 1) is based on assets' after-tax values and 2) correctly reflects the after-tax returns received by and risk borne by the individual investor on assets held in each savings vehicle. Once this is done, (except in an extreme case) there is a clear asset location preference. The optimal asset location is to hold bonds in tax-deferred accounts and Roths and stocks, especially passively-managed stocks, in taxable accounts, while maintaining the target asset allocation. An exception to this general rule is that liquidity reserves must be held in taxable accounts to serve their purpose.

Chapter 6 discussed the investment implications for the optimal sequence in which funds should be withdrawn from the four savings vehicles in retirement. Since the effective tax rate is zero on funds held in tax-deferred accounts and Roths, but positive on assets held in taxable accounts and non-qualified annuities, the rule of thumb is for retirees to withdraw funds from taxable accounts and non-qualified annuities before tax-deferred accounts and Roths. This withdrawal sequence may lengthen a portfolio's longevity by two to five years. If tax rates rise, as many expect, the longevity advantage could be even longer. However, there are exceptions to the rule of thumb. Since the government effectively owns t_n of each dollar in a tax-deferred account, the objective is to look for situations where t_n is unusually low. These low tax rate years may occur: 1) before required minimum distributions (RMDs) begin, 2) in years with large contributions or large medical expenses, and 3) before a general rise in tax rates. This chapter provides additional advice for retirees with a bequeath motive. In particular, if the retiree's tax rate is higher than the beneficiary's then, in general, the retiree should withdraw funds from Roths and leave funds in tax-deferred accounts for the beneficiary, and vice versa.

Other Literature. As previously noted, this book is limited to a discussion of after-tax valuation of assets held in tax-exempt Roths, tax-deferred accounts, taxable accounts, and non-qualified annuities. Most individuals have investments only in these four savings vehicles. This book should cover their situations. However, high net worth clients and clients with special needs often need to consider other vehicles. Brunel (2001 and 2004) goes beyond the material covered in this book. He considers private exchange funds, intergenerational loans, family partnerships, various types of trusts and variable life insurance, as well as the savings vehicles considered in this book. As in this book, his work emphasizes that an asset's location affects its after-tax risk and after-tax return.

YES, VIRGINIA, THERE ARE TAXES!

To date, most financial advisers for individual investors have operated as if taxes do not exist. For example, most financial advisers calculate an individual's asset allocation using the traditional approach, which fails to distinguish between pre-tax and after-tax funds. It considers $1 of pre-tax funds in a tax-deferred account to be as large as $1 of after-tax funds in a Roth or other savings vehicle; it compares apples to oranges. In contrast, the after-tax approach recommended here uses *after-tax* funds in tax-deferred accounts and *after-tax* funds in other savings vehicles to calculate an *after-tax* asset allocation; it compares apples to apples. It is more complex to calculate an individual's after-tax asset allocation, because it usually requires an estimate of the ordinary income tax rate in retirement. In addition, it may require other estimates. However, it is better to face the reality that taxes exist and to make reasonable adjustments for taxes than to pretend that taxes do not exist.

The existence of taxes also has implications for other aspects of private wealth management. For example, it means that the same asset may be an effectively different asset from the investor's perspective when held in different savings vehicles. For example, consider a bond fund with a 4 percent pre-tax return and 6 percent pre-tax standard deviation. If held in a tax-deferred account or Roth the investor's after-tax return and after-tax risk are 4 percent and 6 percent, the same as the pre-tax levels. But, if held in a taxable account by someone in the 25 percent tax bracket, the investor's after-tax return and risk are approximately 3 percent and 4.5 percent. Again, although taxes bring in complexities, it faces the reality that taxes do, indeed, exist. Recognizing this reality will allow a financial adviser to provide asset location advice to improve the after-tax risk and after-tax return on the investor's portfolio. So, although the reality that taxes exist requires more work, it also provides more opportunities for financial advisers to add value to client accounts.

I hope and trust that this book will be a wake-up call to the profession. I hope that it has provided both the rationale for why we should make adjustments for taxes and advice on how to make those adjustments. Even though estimates are required, clients will be better served if financial advisers make tax adjustments based on reasonable estimates than to continue to ignore taxes entirely.

ENDNOTE

[1]*Although there are required minimum distributions from Roth 401(k)s and Roth 403(b)s, they can be effectively avoided by rolling these accounts into a Roth IRA at retirement, because there are no RMDs from a Roth IRA.*

A Theoretical Arguments Associated with Calculating Assets' After-tax Values

This appendix briefly summarizes the development of thought and areas of academic disagreement associated with calculating the after-tax values of assets. These after-tax values should be used to calculate an individual's after-tax asset allocation. In Reichenstein (1998), I was the first to note the failure of the traditional approach to distinguish between $1 of *pre-tax* funds in a tax-deferred account and $1 of *after-tax* funds in a tax-exempt Roth or taxable account. In Reichenstein and Jennings (2003) and Reichenstein (2007a and 2007b), we explained our approach to calculating the after-tax values of funds in Roths, tax-deferred accounts, and taxable accounts.

In Appendix A, we are only concerned with the after-tax value of taxable accounts when the underlying asset's market value equals its cost basis. So, the literature reviewed here concerns the valuation of an asset with a market value of $1 when held in, respectively, a

Roth, a tax-deferred account, and a taxable account (with cost basis equal to $1).

Let us begin with a few simplifying assumptions, so we can quickly focus on developments and areas of agreement and disagreement. Assume the asset is a bond and all of its returns will be realized as interest. The pre-tax return is 5 percent, the length of the investment horizon is ten years, the individual has a 25 percent ordinary income tax rate before retirement, $t = 0.25$, and will have this tax rate in retirement, $t_n = 0.25$.

The central issue is: When calculating an individual's asset allocation, how should we value an asset with a $1 market value if held in, respectively, a Roth, tax-deferred account, and taxable account? In theory, an asset's after-tax value should be equal to its after-tax future value when discounted back to the present at a risk-appropriate discount rate. That is, the after-tax value should equal the discounted after-tax future value.

The after-tax future values of the bond when held in each savings vehicle are as follows:

Tax-exempt Roth: $(1.05)^{10} = \$1.63$ (A1)

Tax-deferred account: $(1.05)^{10}(1 - 0.25) = \$1.22$ (A2)

Taxable account: $(1 + 0.05(1 - 0.25))^{10} = (1.0375)^{10} = \$1.45$ (A3)

The original $1 of after-tax funds in the Roth is worth $1.63 after taxes in ten years. The original $1 of pre-tax funds in the tax-deferred account is worth $(1.05)^{10}$, or $1.63 before taxes, but $1.22 after taxes in ten years. The taxable account grows at the 3.75 percent after-tax rate of return, and the original $1 is worth $1.45 after taxes in ten years. To repeat, the current after-tax values should be equal to the after-tax future values when discounted at the appropriate risk-appropriate discount rate.

The top row of Table A1 summarizes Jennings and Reichenstein's method. We conclude that an asset with $1 market value in a Roth should be valued at \$1, \$1 market value in a tax-deferred account should be valued at $(1 - t_n)$ dollar, (or \$0.75), and \$1 market value in a taxable account (with cost basis = \$1) should be valued at \$1. A detailed explanation of these equations is presented later in this appendix.

Table A1. After-tax Values of Bond with \$1 Market Value in Tax-exempt Roth, Tax-deferred Account, and Taxable Account (When Market Value = Cost Basis)

	Tax-exempt Roth	Tax-deferred Account	Taxable Account (market value = cost basis)
Reichenstein	$(1.05)^{10}/(1.05)^{10}$	$(1.05)^{10}(1 - 0.25)/(1.05)^{10} =$	$(1 + 0.05(1 - 0.25))^{10}/$
*(2007b)**	$= \$1$	$(1 - 0.25) = \$0.75$	$(1 + 0.05(1 - 0.25))^{10} = \$1$
Sibley (2002) &	$(1.05)^{10}/(1 + 0.05(1 - 0.25))^{10}$	$(1.05)^{10}(1-0.25)/(1 + 0.05(1 - 0.25))^{10}$	$(1 + 0.05(1 - 0.25))^{10}/$
Horan (2002)	$= \$1.13$	$= \$0.85$	$(1 + 0.05(1 - 0.25))^{10} = \$1$
Horan (2007)	$(1.05)^{10}/(1.05)^{10}$	$(1.05)^{10}(1 - 0.25)/(1.05)^{10}$	$(1 + 0.05(1 - 0.25))^{10}/$
	$= \$1$	$= (1 - 0.25) = \$0.75$	$(1.05)^{10} = \$0.89$

* Although explained in more detail in Reichenstein (2007c).

The second row summarizes Sibley's (2002) and Horan's (2002) method for valuing a bond with the 5 percent pre-tax return and 10-year investment horizon when the tax rate is 25 percent, $(t = t_n = 0.25)$.[1] Their approach is based on taxable equivalent values, where the taxable equivalent value of a Roth is the amount of funds that must be invested in a taxable account today to produce the same amount of after-tax ending wealth at the end of the investment horizon. The taxable equivalent value of a tax-deferred account is defined in a parallel fashion.

In equation form, Sibley (2002) and Horan (2002) conclude that the \$1 in the Roth should be valued at:

$$(1.05)^{10}/(1 + 0.05(1 - 0.25))^{10} = \$1.13 \qquad (A4)$$

where the numerator of the taxable equivalent value is Equation A1 and the denominator is Equation A3. Therefore, they conclude that, when calculating the asset allocation, the current value of the $1 in a Roth exceeds $1. In a parallel manner, the taxable equivalent value of $1 in a tax-deferred account is:

$$(1.05)^{10} (1 - 0.25)/ (1 + 0.05(1 - 0.25))^{10} = \$0.85 \qquad (A5)$$

which is the ratio of Equations A2 to A3. Depending on rate of return, length of investment horizon and tax rate, this taxable equivalent value may exceed 1, equal 1, or be less than 1.

In Reichenstein (2007b), I critiqued Sibley's (2002) and Horan's (2002) approach. To understand my criticism, notice that these taxable equivalent models are also the present values of the Roth and tax-deferred account's future values *when discounted back at the 3.75 percent after-tax rate of return on the asset when held in a taxable account.* However, as established in Chapter 2, the investor bears all the risk on assets held in a Roth and tax-deferred account. So, the appropriate discount rate is 5 percent, the pre-tax rate of return. It follows that the discounted future value of the Roth is: $(1.05)^{10}/(1.05)^{10} = \$1$. The $1 in the Roth should be valued at $1. The discounted future value of the tax-deferred account is: $(1.05)^{10}(1 - 0.25)/(1.05)^{10} = \$1(1 - 0.25)$. The $1 of pre-tax funds in the tax-deferred account should be valued at $(1 - 0.25)$ after-tax dollar. Similarly, as established in Chapter 2, the investor bears approximately $(1 - t)$ of the risk on assets held in taxable accounts (when market value equals cost basis). So, the appropriate discount rate is $5(1 - 0.25)$, or 3.75 percent, the after-tax rate of return. The discounted future value of the taxable account is: $(1 + 0.05(1 - 0.25))^{10}/(1 + 0.05(1 - 0.25))^{10} = \$1$. The $1 in the taxable account should be valued at $1. A key to my critique is to recognize that the investor bears all the risk on assets held in a Roth and tax-deferred account, whereas the individual bears only $(1 - 0.25)$, or 75 percent of the risk on bonds held in a taxable account.

In a recent article, Horan (2007) now agrees with Jennings and Reichenstein that $1 in a Roth should be valued at $1, while $1 of pre-tax funds in a tax-deferred account should be valued at $(1 - t_n)$

dollar, when calculating an individual's asset allocation. Furthermore, he agrees with us because of the risk-based arguments presented in Reichenstein (2007b). However, he disagrees with the Jennings and Reichenstein approach to valuing $1 in a taxable account (with cost basis = $1). Table A1 summarizes his current position.

To understand his thinking, consider an investment of $1 in a pure discount, ten-year risk-free government bond with a 5 percent yield. After ten years, the ending after-tax values of this bond when held in the Roth and taxable account are, respectively, $(1.05)^{10}$ and $(1.0375)^{10}$. Horan (2007) concludes that the $1 in the taxable account should be valued at $(1.0375)^{10}/(1.05)^{10} = \$0.89$. He discounts the taxable account's future after-tax value by the 5 percent pre-tax rate of return. He believes that the 5 percent risk-free rate is the appropriate rate at which to calculate the discounted present value of the $(1.0375)^{10}$ because the investment is riskless. He says the government cannot share in non-existent risk of the risk-free asset when held in a taxable account.

As explained in Reichenstein (2007c), I disagree with Horan's (2007) approach. I believe that the appropriate discount rate is 3.75 percent, in which case the $1 in a taxable account has a discounted present value of $(1.0375)^{10}/(1.0375)^{10}$ or $1. In the U.S. tax code, when a taxable bond is held in a taxable account, the interest is fully taxable; so, the appropriate discount rate is [5%(1 – 0.25)], or 3.75 percent. In short, the after-tax value of a bond held in a taxable account with market value and cost basis of $1 is $1.

Consider a simple example. An individual takes a $100 bill and deposits it today in a taxable bank savings account. What is its after-tax value today? I conclude it is $100. Horan (2007) concludes that it depends upon risk-free rate of return, expected investment horizon, and marginal tax rate. For a 5 percent return, expected investment horizon of 10 years and 25 percent tax rate, he would conclude that it is worth about $89 today. I disagree.

Finally, as Horan notes, the $1 in risk-free bonds invested in a Roth is assured of having a larger after-tax ending wealth than the $1 invested in a taxable account. Therefore, everyone should prefer the Roth to the taxable account. In my opinion, this tax-exempt Roth's advantage is essentially a tax subsidy. The government limits the size of this subsidy by limiting the size of the annual contribution. However, this tax subsidy does not mean that $1 in a taxable account (with cost basis = $1) should be considered worth less than $1 today.

ENDNOTE

[1]Horan (2002) presents a detailed model to evaluate bonds or stocks. But for the bond in this example, his model reduces to the same model as in Sibley (2002).

B | *Estimating Marginal Tax Rates in Retirement*

This appendix is designed to help financial advisers estimate marginal tax rates in retirement. As discussed in Chapter 1, the after-tax approach to calculating an individual's asset allocation considers each dollar in a tax-deferred account to be like $(1 - t_n)$ dollar in a tax-exempt Roth, where t_n is the marginal tax rate in retirement. By contrast, the traditional approach ignores taxes and thus implicitly assumes tax rates in retirement will be zero. Although an individual's retirement tax rate can only be estimated, the good news is that it is usually easy to improve upon the traditional approach's implicit estimate of zero.

Based on numerous conversations with professionals, there is wide agreement that we will see a general rise in tax rates within the next few years. I can offer no special insight into how much higher tax rates may rise. However, if these forecasts are accurate, marginal tax rates based on today's tax code may be lower bound estimates of tax rates for most Americans in retirement.

In the remainder of this appendix, I will discuss a hump in individuals' and couples' marginal tax rate curves in retirement due to the taxation of Social Security benefits. Usually, when we say someone is in the 25 percent tax bracket, we also mean that he is in the 25 percent marginal tax bracket. That is, if he earns $1 more, then his taxes will increase by $0.25. However, once Social Security benefits begin, there may be a difference between an individual's tax bracket and his marginal tax rate. This feature primarily comes into play with withdrawals from tax-deferred accounts after Social Security benefits have begun.

There is a range in which each additional dollar withdrawn from a tax-deferred account will cause and additional $0.50 or $0.85 of Social Security benefits to be taxable. For withdrawals in that range, each additional dollar withdrawn causes taxable income to increase by $1.50 or $1.85, which causes the marginal tax rate to be either 50 percent or 85 percent higher than the tax bracket. Beyond this range, the maximum of 85 percent of Social Security benefits are already taxable. So, the marginal tax rate on additional withdrawals is again equal to the tax bracket.

Married Couple Filing Jointly. To illustrate the problem, consider a couple that receives $25,000 in Social Security benefits in 2008. The taxation of Social Security benefits depends upon the level of combined income (that is, provisional income) which is defined as the sum of modified adjusted gross income, tax-exempt interest, plus 50 percent of Social Security benefits. The taxable portion of Social Security is the minimum of three amounts: 1) 85 percent of Social Security benefits; 2) 50 percent of benefits plus 85 percent of combined income beyond the second threshold amount; and 3) 50 percent of combined income beyond the first threshold plus 35 percent of combined income beyond the second threshold amount. The first and second threshold amounts are $32,000 and $44,000.

For 2008, the federal tax brackets are 10 percent for taxable income up to $16,050, 15 percent for additional income up to

$65,100, 25 percent for income up to $131,450, 28 percent for income up to $200,300, 33 percent for income up to $357,700, and 35 percent for additional income.

For simplicity, assume their taxable income for the year consists of withdrawals from tax-deferred accounts plus the taxable amount of Social Security benefits.[1] This couple could withdraw up to $19,500 from tax-deferred accounts and no Social Security benefits would be taxable. So, amounts withdrawn through the top of the 10 percent tax bracket and partway through the 15 percent bracket would have marginal tax rates equal to the tax brackets. For the $19,500 withdrawal, their combined income would be $32,000, the first threshold amount.

The next dollar withdrawn causes $0.50 of Social Security benefits to be taxed. So, the dollar withdrawal causes taxable income to increase by $1.50, which causes taxes to increase by $0.225 or [$1.50(0.15)]. The marginal tax rate is 22.5 percent.

The marginal tax rate remains at 22.5 percent through tax-deferred account withdrawals of $31,500, which corresponds to a combined income of $44,000, the second threshold amount. The next dollar withdrawn causes $0.85 of Social Security benefits to be taxed. So, the dollar withdrawal causes taxable income to increase by $1.85, which causes taxes to increase by $0.2775 or [$1.85(0.15)]. The marginal tax rate is 27.75 percent.

The marginal tax rate remains at 27.75 percent through tax-deferred account withdrawals of $46,419, which corresponds to taxable income of $65,100, the top of the 15 percent tax bracket. The next dollar withdrawn causes $0.85 of Social Security benefits to be taxed. So, the dollar withdrawal causes taxable income to increase by $1.85, which causes taxes to increase by $0.4625 or [$1.85(0.25)]. The marginal tax rate is 46.25 percent.

The marginal tax rate remains at 46.25 percent through withdrawals of $49,441, at which time the maximum of 85 percent of Social Security benefits are taxable. The next dollar withdrawn has a marginal tax rate of 25 percent, the same as the tax bracket. The marginal tax rate and tax bracket are the same on additional withdrawals beyond $49,441 (until much later when additional withdrawals affect personal deductions or standard deductions).

Figure B1 summarizes this couple's situation. It shows the amount withdrawn from tax-deferred accounts on the horizontal axis and the marginal tax rate on the vertical axis. The marginal tax rate rises from 10 percent to 15 percent with the tax bracket. But for withdrawals within the range of $19,501 and $49,441, the marginal tax rate rises from 22.5 percent to 27.75 percent and to 46.25 percent. Withdrawals beyond that range have a marginal tax rate equal to

Figure B1. Marginal Tax Rates on Couple's Withdrawals from Tax-deferred Accounts

Withdrawals from Tax-deferred Accounts

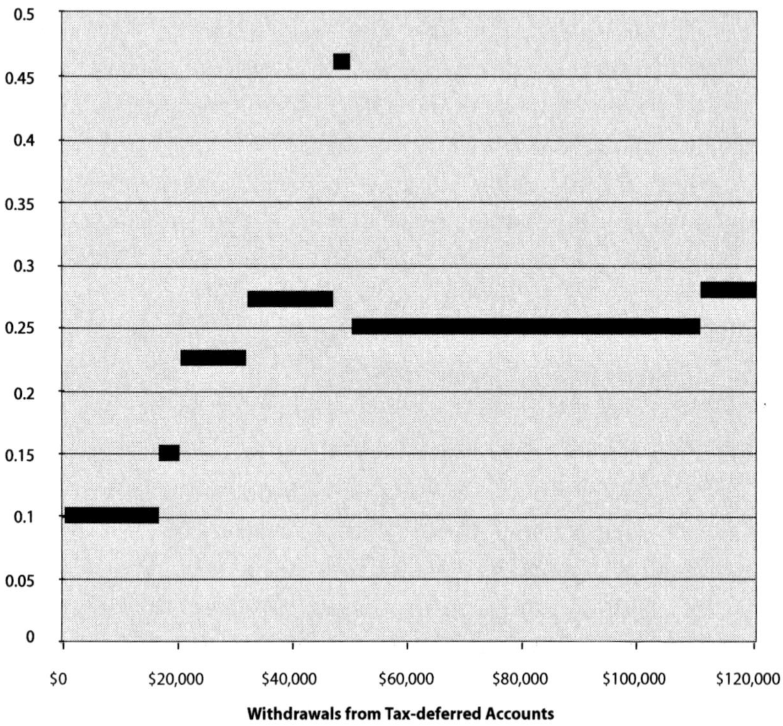

the tax bracket. For example, withdrawals from $49,442 through $110,200 are taxed at 25 percent, where $110,200 corresponds to taxable income at the top of the 25 percent bracket. In short, once Social Security benefits begin, there is a hump in the marginal tax rate schedule for withdrawals from tax-deferred accounts.

In this example, suppose the couple withdrew $30,000 from tax-deferred accounts for 2008. The tax bill associated with this withdrawal would be 0.10($16,050) + 0.15($19,500 − $16,050) + 0.225($30,000 − $19,500). The average of the marginal rates is 15 percent or $4,485/$30,000. That is, by withdrawing $30,000 the couple's tax bill is $4,485 higher than it would have been if they withdrew nothing from tax-deferred accounts. If this marginal tax bill is indicative of their average marginal tax rate per dollar withdrawn from tax-deferred accounts in retirement then t_n would be 0.15.

Suppose this couple had other taxable income of $20,000 and withdrew $100,000 from tax-deferred accounts for 2008. The tax bill associated with this withdrawal would be [0.225($31,500 − $20,000) + 0.2725($46,419 − $31,500) + 0.4625($49,441 − $46,419) + 0.25($110,200 − $49,441) + 0.28($120,000 − $110,200)]. The average of the marginal rates is 26 percent or [$25,984/$100,000]. If this marginal tax bill is indicative of their average marginal tax rate per dollar withdrawn from tax-deferred accounts in retirement then t_n would be 0.26.

Single Individual. Let's consider a single individual who receives $20,000 in Social Security benefits in 2008. For simplicity, assume her taxable income for the year consists of withdrawals from tax-deferred accounts plus the taxable amount of Social Security benefits.[2]

The first and second threshold amounts for singles are $25,000 and $34,000. For 2008, the federal tax brackets are 10 percent for taxable income up to $8,025, 15 percent for additional income up to $32,550, 25 percent for income up to $78,850, 28 percent for income up to $164,550, 33 percent for income up to $357,700, and 35 percent for additional income.

This single individual could withdraw up to $15,000 from tax-deferred accounts and no Social Security benefits would be taxable. So, amounts withdrawn through the top of the 10 percent tax bracket and partway through the 15 percent bracket would have marginal tax rates equal to the tax brackets. For the $15,000 withdrawal, her combined income would be $25,000, the first threshold amount.

The marginal tax rate on withdrawals from $15,001 to $24,000 is 22.5 percent or [$1.50(0.15)], where $24,000 withdrawal from the tax-deferred account corresponds to the second threshold amount. The marginal tax rate on withdrawals from $24,001 to $26,189 is 27.75 percent or [$1.85(0.15)], where a $26,189 withdrawal corresponds to the top of the 15 percent tax bracket. The marginal tax rate on withdrawals from $26,189 to $38,706 is 46.25 percent or [$1.85(0.25)]. For withdrawals from tax-deferred accounts exceeding $38,706, the marginal tax rate is again equal to the tax bracket (until much later when additional withdrawals affect personal deductions or standard deductions).

Figure B2 illustrates the hump in the marginal tax rate curve for this single individual. The hump occurs when each additional dollar withdrawn from tax-deferred accounts causes either an additional $0.50 or $0.85 of Social Security benefits to be taxed. For withdrawals beyond $38,706, the marginal tax rate and tax bracket are the same.

Suppose this single individual withdrew $30,000 from tax-deferred accounts for 2008. The tax bill associated with this withdrawal would be [0.10($8,025) + 0.15($15,000 − $8,025) + 0.225($24,000 − $15,000) + 0.2775($26,189 − $24,000) + 0.4625($30,000 − $26,189)]. The average of the marginal rates is 20.8 percent or [$6,244/$30,000]. That is, by withdrawing $30,000 this individual's tax bill is $6,244 higher than it would have been if they withdrew nothing from tax-deferred accounts. If this marginal tax bill is indicative of her average marginal tax rate per dollar withdrawn from tax-deferred accounts in retirement then t_n would be 0.208.

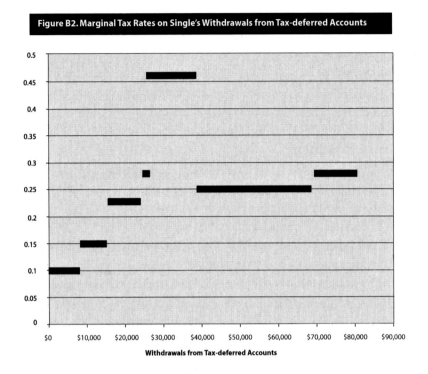

Figure B2. Marginal Tax Rates on Single's Withdrawals from Tax-deferred Accounts

Suppose this single individual had $10,000 of other taxable income and withdrew $20,000 from tax-deferred accounts for 2008. The tax bill associated with this withdrawal would be [0.15($15,000 − $10,000) + 0.225($24,000 − $15,000) + 0.2775($26,189 − $24,000) + 0.4625($30,000 − $26,189)]. The average of the marginal rates is 25.7 percent or [$5,145/$20,000].

When possible, the couple or single individual may refrain from withdrawing funds from tax-deferred accounts that would be subject to the 27.75 percent and 46.25 percent marginal tax rates. For example, depending upon each couple's specific situation, they may be able to limit withdrawals to $31,500 from tax-deferred accounts and make additional withdrawals, as needed, from tax-exempt Roths or taxable accounts. Other couples may have required minimum distributions that are beyond $49,441, in which case they will not be able to avoid this marginal tax rate hump.

Although the topic is beyond the scope of this book, Mahaney and Carlson (2007) discuss a retirement withdrawal strategy that is designed to reduce these problems for some individuals. They believe some individuals would benefit from 1) delaying the start of Social Security benefits until age 70 and 2) withdrawing funds from tax-deferred accounts before age 70. By the time Social Security benefits begin, at 70, the tax-deferred accounts would be substantially reduced, which may prevent required minimum distributions from these accounts from causing the taxation of Social Security benefits.

ENDNOTES

[1] A retiree's income may consist of wages and salaries, capital gains and dividends, Social Security benefits, and withdrawals from tax-deferred accounts. In general, the level of withdrawals from tax-deferred accounts is the income category most under the taxpayer's control. The required minimum distribution amount, if any, sets the minimum withdrawal amount each year, but retirees may withdraw additional amounts at their discretion. Thus retirees should manage withdrawals from tax-deferred accounts in a tax-efficient manner.

[2] See endnote 1.

After-tax Valuation of Assets Held in Taxable Accounts and Non-qualified Annuities with Built-in Deferred Returns

In theory, an asset's after-tax value should equal its after-tax future value when discounted back to the present at a risk-appropriate discount rate. That is, the after-tax value should equal the discounted after-tax future value.

Let us begin with a simple example. Consider a bond with a market value of $1 and cost basis of $1. If the pre-tax return is 5 percent, ordinary income tax rate is 25 percent, and the investment horizon is 8 years, then the after-tax future value is $(1 + 0.05(1 - 0.25))^8 = \$1.34$. From Chapter 2, the investor bears 75 percent or $(1 - 0.25)$ of the bond's risk. So, the appropriate discount rate is $[5\%(1 - 0.25)]$ or 3.75 percent. Mathematically, the present value of the after-tax future value is $[(1 + 0.05(1 - 0.25))^8/(1 + 0.05(1 - 0.25))^8 = \$1]$, where the numerator is the after-tax future value and the denominator is 1 plus the risk-appropriate discount rate. That is, the after-tax value of this bond today is $1. Although it is clear that the after-tax value of a bond with a market value and cost basis of $1 is $1, we can follow the logic in this example to value assets with embedded deferred returns. We will begin with the valuation of a stock with an embedded unrealized capital gain and then consider the value of a non-qualified annuity with embedded deferred returns.

Stock with embedded gain. Suppose a stock has a market value of $20,000 and cost basis of $16,000. What is its after-tax value for an investor who is in the 25 percent ordinary income tax bracket and 15 percent capital gain tax bracket? This example comes from Chapter 3, where we considered its value for a trader, active investor, passive investor, and exempt investor.

The after-tax values for the trader, active investor, and exempt investor are the market value less the tax liability on the embedded gain. Since the tax liability for the trader on the $4,000 gain would be $1,000, or [$4,000(0.25)], the after-tax value is $19,000. Since the tax liability for the active investor would be $600, or [$4,000(0.15)], the after-tax value is $19,400. Since there would be no tax liability for the exempt investor, the after-tax value is $20,000.

For the passive investor, the after-tax value is $19,400, or $20,000 market value less the tax liability of $600. Since the tax liability will not be paid for, potentially, several years, it is not immediately evident that this stock's after-tax value is $19,400. An example will illustrate that its after-tax value should be $19,400, the value as if the gain was realized today and taxed at 15 percent.

Suppose the stock with a market value of $20,000 and cost basis of $16,000 has a 6 percent return and all returns are in the form of capital gains. The tax rate at liquidation is 15 percent and the investment horizon is 10 years. The after-tax future value will be $32,844. The future market value before considering taxes is [$20,000(1.06)^{10}], or $35,817. After paying taxes at 15 percent on the $19,817 gain ($35,817 less the $16,000 cost basis), the after-tax future value is $32,844.

If the stock was liquidated today and the embedded gain taxed at 15 percent, its after-tax value would be $19,400. So, by deferring the recognition of the gain for 10 years, the after-tax value grows from $19,400 to $32,844. This is a 5.406 percent after-tax rate of return. That is, $19,400(1.05406)^{10} = $32,844$. The 5.406 percent returns means the investor receives 90.10 percent of returns, [5.406%/6%]. So, the effective tax rate is 9.9 percent or $(1 - 0.9010)$. Since the effective tax rate is 9.9 percent, the risk-appropriate discount rate is $[6\%(1 - 0.099)]$, or 5.406 percent. Mathematically, $19,400(1.05406)^{10} = $19,400(1 + 0.06(1 - 0.099))^{10} = $32,844$. So the present value of the after-tax future value is $32,844/(1.05406)^{10} = $32,844/(1 + 0.06(1 - 0.099))^{10} = $19,400$.

This example shows that after-tax value of a stock with embedded capital gains is the market value less the tax liability on the embedded gain if the gain was realized today and taxed at t_c, the long-term capital gain tax rate. If we changed the assumed return or length of investment horizon we would change the portion of return received by the investor and the effective tax rate. However, the after-tax future value when discounted at the discount rate that reflects that effective tax rate would still be $19,400.

The next section shows that the same logic applies to valuing assets with tax-deferred returns when held in a non-qualified annuity.

Non-qualified annuity with embedded tax-deferred returns. The same logic applies to calculating the after-tax value of an asset with embedded deferred returns when held in a non-qualified annuity. The after-tax value is the market value less the tax liability if the deferred returns were recognized today and taxed at t_n.

Assume the annuity's market value is $20,000 and cost basis is $16,000. It will be liquidated after earning 6 percent per year for 15 years and the tax rate at liquidation will be 25 percent. The after-tax future value is $39,948. The future market value before considering taxes is $[$20,000(1.06)^{15}]$, or $47,931. After paying taxes at 25 percent on the $31,931 of deferred returns ($47,931 less the $16,000 cost basis), the after-tax future value is $39,948.

If the asset was liquidated today and deferred returns were taxed at 25 percent, its after-tax value would be $19,000. So, by deferring the recognition of the deferred returns for 15 years, the after-tax value grows from $19,000 to $39,948. This is a 5.079 percent after-tax rate of return. That is, $19,000(1.05079)^{15} = $39,948$. The 5.079 percent return means the investor receives 84.65 percent of returns, [5.079%/6%]. So, the effective tax rate is 15.35 percent, or (1 − 0.8465). Since the effective tax rate is 15.35 percent, the risk-appropriate discount rate is [6%(1 − 0.1535)], or 5.079 percent. Mathematically, $19,000(1.05079)^{15} = $19,000(1 + 0.06(1 − 0.1535))^{15} = $39,948$. The present value of the after-tax future value is $39,948/(1.05079)^{15} = $39,948/(1 + 0.06(1 − 0.1535))^{15} = $19,000$.

This example shows that after-tax value of an asset held in a non-qualified annuity with deferred returns is the market value less the tax liability on the embedded deferred returns if they were realized today and taxed at t_n, the ordinary income tax rate. If we changed the assumed return or length of investment horizon we would change the portion of return received by the investor and the effective tax rate. However, the after-tax future value when discounted at the discount rate that reflects that effective tax rate would still be $19,000.

References

Brunel, Jean. (2001) "Asset Location—The Critical Variable: A Case Study." *Journal of Wealth Management*. Summer. pp. 27–43.

Brunel, Jean. (2004) "The Tax Efficient Portfolio." in *The Investment Think Tank*, edited by Harold Evensky and Deena Katz. Bloomberg Press: Princeton, NJ. pp. 5–16.

Dammon, Robert M.; Spatt, Chester S.; and Zhang, Harold H.. (2004) "Optimal Asset Location and Allocation with Taxable and Tax-Deferred Investing." *Journal of Finance*. June. pp. 999–1037.

Horan, Stephen M. (2002) "After-tax Valuation of Tax Sheltered Assets." *Financial Services Review*. Vol. 11, no. 3. Fall. pp. 253–276.

Horan, Stephen M. (2007) "Applying After-tax Asset Allocation." *Journal of Wealth Management*. Vol. 10, no. 2. Fall. pp. 84–93.

Horan, Stephen M. (2006) "Optimal Withdrawal Strategies for Retirees with Multiple Savings Accounts." *Journal of Financial Planning.* November. pp. 62–75.

Horan, Stephen M. (2006b) "Withdrawal Location with Progressive Tax Rates." *Financial Analysts Journal.* November/December. pp. 77–87.

Jeffrey, Robert H. and Arnott, Robert D. (1993) "Is Your Alpha Big Enough to Cover Its Taxes?" *Journal of Portfolio Management.* Spring. pp. 15–25.

Jennings, William W. and Reichenstein, William. (2006) *The Literature of Private Wealth Management.* Research Foundation of the CFA Institute. www.cfapubs.org/doi/pdf/10.2470/rflr.v1.n3.4362.

Mahaney, James I. and Carlson, Peter C. (2007) "Rethinking Social Security Claiming in a 401(k) World." Pension Research Council Working Paper 2007-18. Wharton School, University of Pennsylvania.

Markowitz, Harry. (1952). "Portfolio Selection." *Journal of Finance.* Vol. 7, no. 1. pp. 77–91.

Reichenstein, William. (2006a) "After-tax Asset Allocation." *Financial Analysts Journal.* July/August. pp. 14–19.

Reichenstein, William. (2003a) "Allocation During Retirement: Adding Annuities to the Mix." *AAII Journal,* November. pp. 3–9.

Reichenstein, William. (2001a) "Asset Allocation and Asset Location Decisions Revisited." *Journal of Wealth Management.* Summer. pp. 16–26.

William Reichenstein. (2007a) "Calculating After-tax Asset Allocation is Key to Determining Risk, Returns, and Asset Location." *Journal of Financial Planning.* July. pp. 66–77.

Reichenstein, William. (1998) "Calculating a Family's Asset Mix." *Financial Services Review*. Vol. 7, no. 3. pp. 195–206.

Reichenstein, William. (2007b) "Implications of Principal, Risk, and Returns Sharing across Savings Vehicles." *Financial Services Review*. Vol. 16, no. 1. pp. 1–17.

Reichenstein, William. (2007c) "Note on 'Applying After-tax Asset Allocation.'" *Journal of Wealth Management*. Fall. pp. 94–97.

Reichenstein, William. (2003b) "Retirement Planning: Annuities and When They Make Sense." *AAII Journal*. July. pp. 23–28.

Reichenstein, William. (2006b) "Sequencing of Accounts to Tap in Retirement." Trends and Issues. TIAA-CREF Institute, October. See www.tiaa-crefinstitute.org/research/trends.

Reichenstein, William. (2006c) "Withdrawal Strategies to Make Your Nest Egg Last Longer." *AAII Journal*. November. pp. 5–11.

Reichenstein, William and Jennings, William W. (2003) *Integrating Investments and the Tax Code*. John Wiley & Sons, Inc.: New York, NY.

Sibley, M. (2002). "On the Valuation of Tax-advantaged Retirement Accounts." *Financial Services Review*. Vol. 11, no.3. Fall. pp. 233–251.

Spitzer, John J. and Singh, Sandeep. (2006) "Extending Retirement Payouts by Optimizing the Sequence of Withdrawals." *Journal of Financial Planning*. April. pp. 52–61.

Waltenberger, Alicia; Rothermich, Douglas; and Reichenstein, William. (2006) "The Expanding 'Roth' Retirement Account." TIAA-CREF Institute, March. See www.tiaa-crefinstitute.org/research/trends/tr030106.html.

In the Presence of Taxes: Applications of After-tax Asset Valuations

Index

401(k), vii, 1–2, 5–9, 14, 22, 29, 43–45, 50–53, 55–57, 60, 64, 75, 77, 89, 92, 99, 101, 124

active investor, 14, 16–17, 22, 23–25, 31, 37–38, 60–64, 66, 69, 78, 88–89, 100, 120

adjusted gross income (AGI), 32, 41, 53, 56, 84, 86, 95

after-tax asset allocation, vii, 1–3, 5, 8–11, 23, 27–28, 32–37, 39–41, 44, 65, 80, 96, 100, 103, 105, 123–125

after-tax future value, 106, 119–122

asset allocation, vii, 1–2, 5, 8–11, 27–29, 33–37, 39, 44, 54, 57, 59, 61–63, 65–67, 71–73, 76, 80, 96, 101, 103, 106–107, 109, 111, 123–124

asset location, 1–2, 5, 37, 59, 61, 63, 65–68, 70–73, 80, 96, 100–103, 103, 123–124 bond, vii, 2, 6, 8–10, 13–16, 18, 20–25, 29–30, 32–38, 47, 54, 59–73, 76–80, 82, 88–91, 95–96, 100–101, 103, 106–110, 119–120

Brunel, Jean, 3, 102, 123

Canada, 35, 44–46

cash flows, 10, 28

certificate of deposit (CD), 69–70

correlation coefficient, 61–64

cost basis, 15, 17–18, 20, 24–25, 29–32, 34–37, 40, 64, 85, 105–110, 119–121

Dammon, Spatt, and Zhang (2004), 72, 123

death benefit, 25–26, 69–70, 91–92

discount rate, 106, 108–109, 119–122

dividend yield, 16–17, 25

dividends, 14, 16–18, 20, 60, 72, 78, 100, 118

effective tax rate, 8, 15, 19, 21–23, 25, 47, 49, 57, 64, 66–69, 72, 75, 77–78, 80, 82–85, 88–89, 102, 121–122

embedded capital gain, 38–40, 121

embedded capital loss, 31, 40

embedded deferred return, 3, 120–122

embedded gain, 30–31, 120–121

embedded unrealized capital gain, 39, 120,

Evensky, Harold, 3, 123

exempt investor, 14, 17, 21–25, 31, 69, 78, 84, 120

expected return, 15, 17, 37–38, 61–62, 64

Gordon, Robert, 3

hedge fund, 69–70

Horan, Stephen, 3–4, 76, 87, 107–110, 123–124

Horvitz, Jeffrey, 3, 11

interest-bearing asset, 69–70

IRA, vii, 1–2, 5–9, 14, 20, 33–35, 43, 45, 53–54, 77, 84, 86, 89, 93–94

Jennings, William, 1, 3–4, 26, 28–29, 105–106, 108–109, 124–125

Katz, Deena, 3, 123

long-term capital gain rate, 16, 18, 19, 23, 25, 35, 39, 40

marginal tax rate, vii, 2–3, 6–8, 10–11, 43, 47, 50–51, 54, 56, 76, 86–87, 93–94, 99–101, 109, 111–118

market value, vii, 1, 8, 13–15, 17, 20, 24–25, 27–41, 62–64, 85, 91–92, 100–101, 105–109, 119–122

Markowitz, Harry, 61, 124

mean variance optimization, 2, 54, 59, 61–64, 71, 73, 101

Milevsky, Moshe, 3

modified adjusted gross income (MAGI), 56, 112

mortgage-backed security (MBS), 10, 28

non-qualified annuity, 18, 20–21, 24–25, 29, 31–32, 35–36, 39–40, 41, 61, 64–65, 68, 89, 92, 120–122

ordinary income tax rate, 13–16, 20–24, 29, 32–35, 37, 39–41, 45, 60, 67, 69, 78, 103, 106, 119, 122

passive investor, 14, 17, 19, 22–25, 31, 69, 78, 85, 120

portfolio, vii, 2, 6, 32–38, 59, 61–66, 71–72, 76–83, 92, 95–97, 102–103, 123–124

Poterba, James, 3

prepayment rate, 10, 28

present value, 108–109, 119, 121–122

real estate investment trust (REIT), 69–70

realized loss, 23, 32, 40

Reichenstein, William, vi, 4, 14, 26, 28–29, 54, 60, 72, 76, 105–109, 124–125

required minimum distribution (RMD), 53, 55–56, 71, 80, 83–84, 86, 93–95, 101–102, 104, 118

Retirement Accounts First strategy, 79–82, 95

risk, vii, 5, 10, 13–18, 24–25, 54, 59–68, 72, 91, 100–103, 106, 108–109, 119–122, 124–125

risk tolerance (RT), 36, 62–66

Rogers, Douglas, 3

Roth, 2, 7, 10–11, 13–15, 21–25, 28–29, 32–35, 39–41, 43–50, 52–56, 59–73, 75–80, 85, 87–90, 92–94, 97, 99–103, 105–111, 117, 125

Roth 401(k), vii, 7, 39, 43, 45, 50–53, 55–57, 77, 89, 101, 104

Roth IRA, vii, 1–2, 5–9, 14, 22, 33–35, 43, 45, 47, 51–57, 60, 64, 75, 77, 84, 89, 93–94, 99, 104

Shoven, John, 3
Sialm, Clemens, 3
Sibley, William, 3, 107–108, 110, 125
SIMPLE, 56–57
Singh, Sandeep, 3, 76, 87, 125
Spitzer, John, 3, 76, 87, 125
standard deviation (SD), 15, 17, 61–62, 64, 103
stock, vii, 2–3, 6, 8–10, 13–14, 16–25, 30–39, 47, 54, 59–73, 76–80, 82–85, 88–92, 95–97, 100–101, 110, 120
Tax Free Savings Account (TFSA), 45–46
tax liability, 27, 30–33, 36, 38–41, 120–122
tax oblivious, 2, 54, 61, 71, 101
Taxable Accounts First strategy, 79–83, 95
trader, 14, 16, 22–25, 31, 67, 69, 120
traditional approach, 1, 9–11, 27–28, 33–37, 39, 62–63, 65, 103, 105, 111
U.S. savings bond, 20, 38
undeveloped land, 38
United States (U.S.), 34–35, 44, 46, 56, 83, 109
unrealized capital gain, 3, 23, 30, 39, 93–94
volatility, 25
Wilcox, Jarrod, 3
withdrawal strategy, 76, 118